PHOTOSHOP POWER SHORTCUTS

MICHAEL NINNESS

Photoshop Power Shortcuts

Copyright © 2000 by Hayden Books

All rights reserved. No part of this book shall be reproduced, stored in a retrieval system, or transmitted by any means, electronic, mechanical, photocopying, recording, or otherwise, without written permission from the publisher. No patent liability is assumed with respect to the use of the information contained herein. Although every precaution has been taken in the preparation of this book, the publisher and author assume no responsibility for errors or omissions. Neither is any liability assumed for damages resulting from the use of the information contained herein.

International Standard Book Number: 0-7897-2172-4

Library of Congress Catalog Card Number: 99-65648

Printed in the United States of America

First Printing: October 1999

01 00 99 4 3 2 1

Trademarks

All terms mentioned in this book that are known to be trademarks or service marks have been appropriately capitalized. Hayden Books cannot attest to the accuracy of this information. Use of a term in this book should not be regarded as affecting the validity of any trademark or service mark.

Warning and Disclaimer

Every effort has been made to make this book as complete and as accurate as possible, but no warranty or fitness is implied. The information provided is on an "as is" basis. The author and the publisher shall have neither liability nor responsibility to any person or entity with respect to any loss or damages arising from the information contained in this book.

PUBLISHER
John Pierce

EXECUTIVE EDITOR
Beth Millett

MANAGING EDITOR
Thomas F. Hayes

PROJECT EDITOR
Karen S. Shields

COPY EDITOR
Julie McNamee

INDEXER
Greg Pearson

PROOFREADER
Jeanne Clark

TECHNICAL EDITOR
Kate Binder

TEAM COORDINATOR
Julie Otto

INTERIOR DESIGN
Anne Jones

COVER DESIGN
Karen Ruggles

COPY WRITER
Eric Borgert

PRODUCTION
Eric S. Miller

Rev Up in Adobe Photoshop with Fuel-Efficient Key Commands!

Tell me: Did you actually read the owner's manual after you bought your most recent new car? Hmmm? So, do you know how to open all the windows at the same time—simply by pressing those two little buttons? Can you activate the automatic tint on your windshield to reduce glare or increase brightness and contrast? And hey, how about that super-nifty hands-free auto-pilot feature that controls ALL the functions of your car?

Let me guess: You didn't even know these things were possible, and you're thinking, "Why didn't I read the manual?" Well, if you had read the manual, you would know that I'm totally out of my mind and that none of these automotive shortcuts really exist.

Now you're probably asking yourself, "What does this have to do with that great software, Adobe Photoshop and Adobe ImageReady?" (The answer to this question, by the way, is an astonishing revelation that only a few can comprehend.) But the point is, IF these amazing things were possible with your car, then Michael Ninness would know them. But, unfortunately, since his driver's license was revoked, Michael's had to focus his talents elsewhere. And so, combining his interest in Adobe Photoshop with his long days spent at the county courthouse, Michael has mastered every Adobe Photoshop and Adobe ImageReady shortcut known to man and mechanic and put them together in this one convenient book, *Photoshop Power Shortcuts*.

I can personally say that *Photoshop Power Shortcuts* presents every Adobe Photoshop and Adobe ImageReady shortcut in the known universe. (That is, until the universe changes—and to cover that possibility, you can find updates at `http://www.hayden.com/powershortcuts`.) So, at this moment in time, this book literally has it all. And if you're the type who wants to get where you're going fast in your car—whoops! I mean fast with Adobe Photoshop—then this unique book is the single reference you should have within close reach when you're working in Adobe Photoshop.

I produce a lot of tips and techniques for using Adobe software, and I know this book will come in handy for me. (Actually, I'm not sure why I never thought of putting this book together myself…) I'm always trying to remember Photoshop shortcuts. I know them for a while, but if I don't use them often or if I'm away from the program for any length of time, I forget a lot. With its easy-to-use compendium of shortcuts, *Photoshop Power Shortcuts* is a great resource to have right at the fingertips. I'm already finding that I can't live without it.

As I always say: Good design! Good design! Good design! You can never fail if you create something that's designed well! *Photoshop Power Shortcuts* takes a simple idea, packages it in a good design, and—BINGO!—it's a winner!

I know I won't ever double-click Adobe Photoshop again without it.

Russell Preston Brown
Senior Creative Director and Photoshop Evangelist
Adobe Systems Incorporated

About the Author

Michael Ninness is a Senior Product Manager for Web Graphics at Adobe Systems Incorporated. Before joining Adobe, he was the Group Product Manager for Imaging Solutions at Extensis Corporation. He has spent the last 10 years as a graphic designer, instructor, author, and industry guru. He is a featured speaker at national-level events, such as MacWorld and the Photoshop, Web Design, and QuarkXPress conferences produced by Thunder Lizard Productions (`www.thunderlizard.com`). He is also the author of *Photoshop 5 Web Magic*.

Dedication

For my niece Tracy Lynn and her two pals, Thelma and Louise.

Acknowledgements

Special thanks to tech editor Kate Binder, who reviewed the database more times than anyone can count and took screen shots 'til her fingers were numb.

Tell Us What You Think!

As the reader of this book, you are our most important critic and commentator. We value your opinion and want to know what we're doing right, what we could do better, what areas you'd like to see us publish in, and any other words of wisdom you're willing to pass our way.

As a Publisher for Hayden Books, I welcome your comments. You can fax, email, or write me directly to let me know what you did or didn't like about this book—as well as what we can do to make our books stronger.

Please note that I cannot help you with technical problems related to the topic of this book, and that due to the high volume of mail I receive, I might not be able to reply to every message.

When you write, please be sure to include this book's title and author as well as your name and phone or fax number. I will carefully review your comments and share them with the author and editors who worked on the book.

Fax: 317-581-4666

Email: hayden@mcp.com

Mail: John Pierce
Publisher
Hayden Books
201 West 103rd Street
Indianapolis, IN 46290 USA

Contents

Tools 25

Selections 285

Introduction

Introduction

How many of you use Photoshop so much that you think of it as an operating system?

I got the idea for this book from all the sessions I have done over the years at various Photoshop conferences and seminars. Invariably, after I'm finished with a session, I am flooded by people coming up to me at the stage asking, "Now what was that keyboard shortcut you showed us again?"

As you will see in this book, there are more than 600 keyboard shortcuts in Photoshop! A large amount of them can not be found in the manual that comes with Photoshop, nor are they listed in Photoshop's menus. This book lists them all, and more importantly, indexes them in an accessible way. Chances are there is a shortcut, or several, that you could be using—instead of doing things the way you do them today—that could literally save you minutes, even hours, a day.

There are several ways to use this book, but you will probably find it is most useful when you want to see if there is a shortcut for a particular tool or operation that you use a lot. Simply look in the index for that tool or command and see what page the shortcut is listed on. The shortcut for both Macintosh and Windows versions of Photoshop will be listed.

And don't forget, if you can't remember what that one keyboard shortcut is, just hold down the entire left side of your keyboard and see what happens. Just don't EVER press (Macintosh: Cmd-Option-Shift-R) [Windows: Ctrl+Alt+Shift+R]! That reformats your hard drive...

:)

The 15 Tips You Must Learn. Quicker.

Your ultimate goal when mastering the Photoshop user interface is to make it as transparent as possible. When you want to switch to a different tool, change a brush size, or open a dialog box, you shouldn't have to stop what you're doing; waste your time looking for the tool, palette, menu item, and so on; choose it; and then come back to where you were. The true Photoshop gods simply press a key or key combination, and things just happen.

Hundreds of keyboard shortcuts are listed in this book. Don't try to memorize all of them all at once—you'll freak and get overwhelmed. Start by looking at the following Top 15 list. Some of the items in the list are not single shortcuts, but are a category of shortcuts that you should commit to memory. Master one category, work them into your workflow, and then move on to the next category. After awhile, something magical happens: The Photoshop UI becomes a subconscious thing and you experience Pixel Nirvana. You think Paintbrush tool, and your finger instinctively presses the B key, without you having to actually think the B key or even look at the keyboard.

This list is presented in the order that I recommend people memorize them, but of course, your mind probably works differently than mine, so do what works for you.

1. **Tool Shortcuts**

   Every tool has a letter assigned to it. To select the particular tool you want, just press its letter on the keyboard. Most of the shortcuts make sense, like M for the Marquee tool, E for the Eraser tool, and so on. Some tools on the toolbar actually house several options. To cycle through a tool slot's options, simply use Shift+ the letter for the tool. The real power behind learning these particular shortcuts first is that when you know them all, it doesn't matter if the toolbar is actually open or not because you will be able to get to the tool you want at any time. See page 26 to see a key to all the tools and their respective shortcuts.

2. **Brush Size**

   Changing your brush size on-the-fly without moving your mouse from the area that you are currently using the brush on is a huge timesaver and keeps your brain centered on the task at hand. To select next brush, press]. To select previous brush, press [. To select the first brush, press Shift + [and to select the last brush, press Shift +].

3. **Move Tool**

   The Move tool is arguably the most-used tool in Photoshop. To that end, Adobe has made it easy to temporarily switch to that tool when you are in any other tool. Just hold down the (Cmd) [Ctrl] key while using any other tool.

4. **Palette Shortcuts**

   Just like the tools, every palette has a keystroke assigned to it to make showing and hiding palettes quick and efficient. Learn them. Until you have them memorized, just keep hitting any of the F5 through the F9 keys (F5 through F11 for ImageReady 2.0) until you see the palette tab you are looking for. After awhile, you will have them memorized and you won't think about it any more.

   Also, don't waste a lot of time opening and closing and moving palettes around the screen. I arrange them on the screen once and then leave them open at all times, always keeping them in the same position. That way, I always know where to look when I need to interact with a specific palette, and they don't get lost behind each other. If they get in the way, I just hit the Tab key to hide them, and then Tab again to bring them back.

   See page 12 for a recommended arrangement for the palettes. See pages 13–23 for a key to all the palettes and their respective shortcuts.

5. **Navigation Shortcuts**

   Panning and zooming around an image can be a huge waste of time. Learn how to do it efficiently, and then raise your rates or ask for a raise. See pages 60-65 for all the navigation shortcuts. You'll notice that there are a lot of them. Pick one or two at a time to add to your repertoire, memorize them, and then add a couple more. After awhile, you will begin to appreciate the subtle differences between them and, more importantly, when to use one over another.

6. **Contextual Menus**

   The typical Photoshop user often overlooks this particular category of shortcuts, which is too bad, because there is a contextual menu for just about everything in Photoshop. All the tools, and most of the palettes, have contextual menus that provide quick access to options and commands specific to that tool or palette. One of my favorites is the contextual menu for a Type layer that gives me a quick pop-up menu from which I can rasterize the type by choosing Render Layer. To access a contextual menu, hold down the Ctrl key on the Mac, or the right-mouse button on Windows. See pages 326–344 for a key to all the available contextual menus.

7. **Exchange Foreground and Background Colors; reset Foreground and Background back to default black and white**

   X for exchange, D for default. Next.

8. **Fill Commands**

   Okay, it's time to face the fact that the Bucket tool is for wimps! Learn the Fill command shortcuts to quickly change the color of a selection or a layer. See pages 84–85 for all the Fill command shortcuts.

9. **Layer Shortcuts**

   There are far too many shortcuts for creating, selecting, viewing, and moving layers to list here. The more of these you know the more of a pro you will be. See pages 106–134 for the Layer shortcuts.

10. **Merging Layers**

    After you master creating, selecting, viewing, and moving layers, you will want to know the quick ways to merge and delete them, particularly the shortcuts for deleting multiple layers at once. See pages 109 and 120 for the shortcuts for merging and deleting layers.

11. **Opacity Shortcuts**

    Type a single number; the opacity changes to a 10% increment. Type two numbers quickly; the opacity changes to a 1% increment. For example, if you press 6, you get 60%. If you press 66 quickly, you get 66%. Just don't type 666—that reformats your hard drive. If you have the Move tool selected, you will be changing the opacity of the active layer. If you have a painting tool selected, you are changing the opacity of that tool. Otherwise, you will be changing the opacity of the active layer.

12. **Multiple Undo/Redo Shortcuts**

    Learn these. Quicker. See page 21 for the multiple undo/redo shortcuts.

13. **Revert**

    F12. Learn it, live it, love it.

14. **Image→Adjust Dialog Shortcuts**

    Levels, Curves, Color Balance, and Hue/Saturation. You are in these dialog boxes everyday! They all have shortcuts to open, reopen, and cancel them. Turn to pages 90-91 for these everyday dialog box shortcuts.

15. **Reset Dialog Boxes**

    When you make a mistake when editing the values in a dialog box and you just want to start over from the beginning, don't bother clicking the Cancel button and reopening the dialog box. Just hold down the (Option) [Alt] key, and the Cancel button changes to a Reset button.

PART ONE

Photoshop

Palettes

Palettes

Working Efficiently with Palettes

You know you are living large when you are working in Photoshop with dual monitors—one for the document window, and one for all the palettes. For those of us who don't have two monitors, my general strategy for arranging the palettes is to group them in such a way that I can access any and all of the palettes using the default Function key assignments. In other words, not every palette has a Function key assigned to it, but as long as a given palette is grouped with a palette that does have a Function key assigned to it, you can get to that palette without having to pull down the menu.

When I watch people working in Photoshop, two of the most inefficient habits I see include constantly moving palettes all over the screen and overlapping the palettes so that sometimes a palette gets hidden behind another palette. I overcome this by arranging the palettes on the screen the way you see them in the figure, and then leaving them there. I never (hardly) move them from these positions. I just leave them open all the time. If they are in the way, I simply press the Tab key to hide the palettes and get them out of the way.

The other advantage of never moving the palettes is that if I do actually close a palette or palettes, I always know where a given palette is going to be when I reopen it and don't have to waste time looking for it.

Show or Hide All Palettes

Both: Tab

Show or Hide All But the Tool Palette

Both: Shift+Tab

Remove the Focus of a Numeric Edit Field in a Palette

Both: Enter or Return

Show or Hide the Navigator Palette

Menu: Window→Show/Hide Navigator

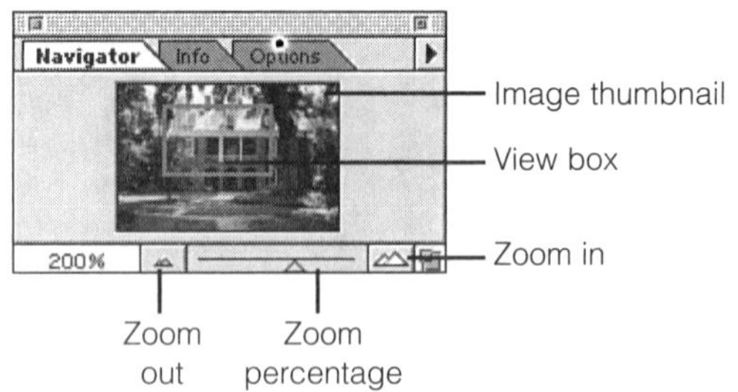

Show or Hide the Info Palette

Menu: Window→Show/Hide Info

Both: F8

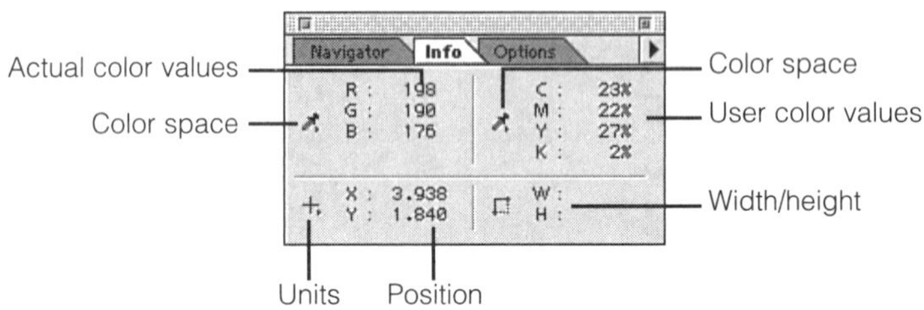

Change the Unit of Measure in the Info Palette

Mouse: Click on cross-hair icon pop-up

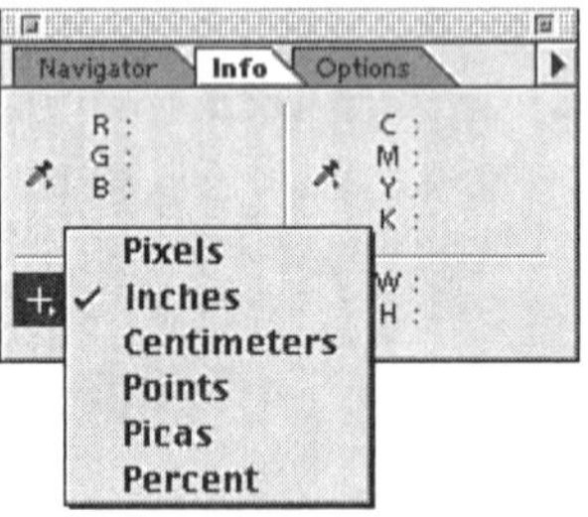

Change the Color Mode of Readout

Mouse: Click on eyedropper icon pop-up

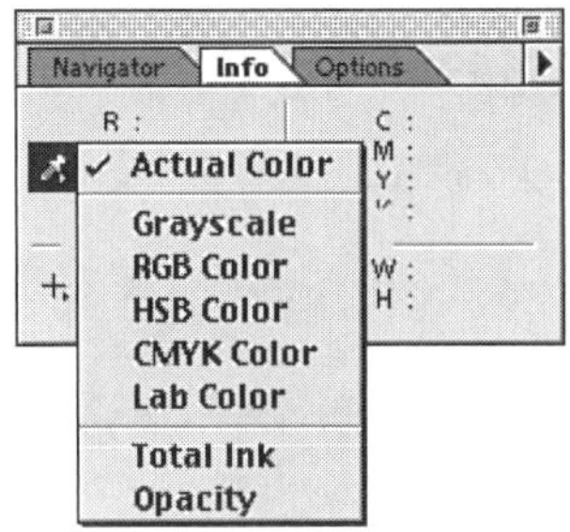

Open the Options Palette

Menu: Window→Show/Hide Options

Both: Enter or Return

Mouse: Double-click on a tool

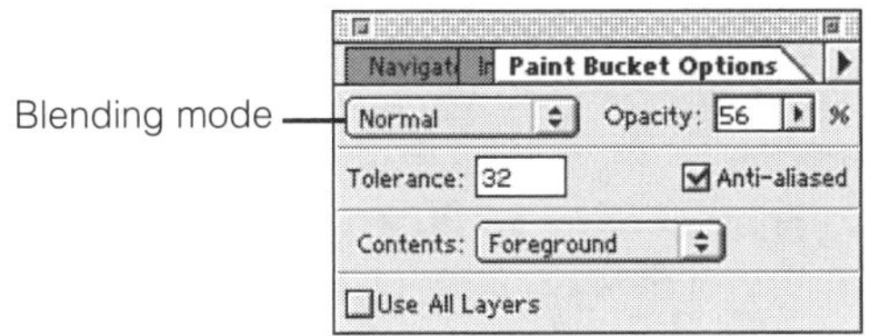

Show or Hide the Color Palette

Menu: Window→Show/Hide Color

Both: F6

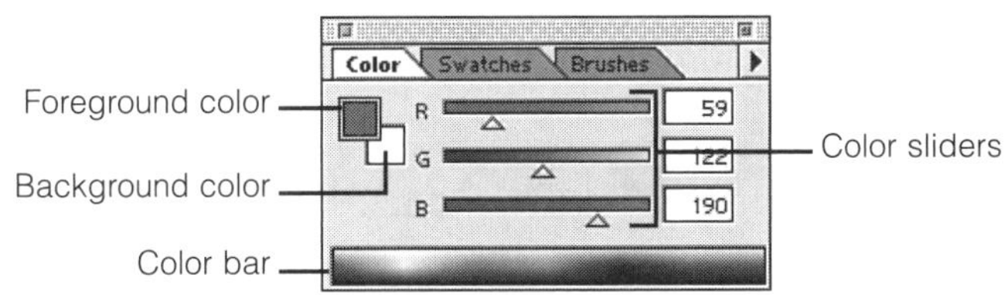

Select Background Color (in the Color Palette)

Mac: Option-Click on color ramp

Win: Alt+Click on color ramp

Cycle Through Color Ramps in the Color Palette

Mouse: Shift+Click on color bar

The default color bar at the bottom of the Color palette displays the RGB color spectrum for quick selection of colors without having to open the Color Picker dialog box. You can change the ramp to display an RGB, CMYK, Grayscale, or Current Colors color ramp.

Open the Color Bar Dialog Box

Mac: Cmd-Click on color bar

Win: Ctrl+Click on color bar

The default color bar at the bottom of the Color palette displays the RGB color spectrum for quick selection of colors without having to open the Color Picker dialog box. You can change the ramp to display the CMYK Spectrum or a Grayscale color ramp. If you choose the Current Colors option from the pop-up menu, a gradient ramp of the current foreground and background colors appears. New to Photoshop 5.5: You can now choose the Make Ramp Web Safe option!

Choose a Specific Color Bar

Mac: Ctrl-Click on color bar

Win: Right-click on color bar

This displays a contextual menu of the four different display choices for the color bar, plus the option to choose Make Ramp Web Safe.

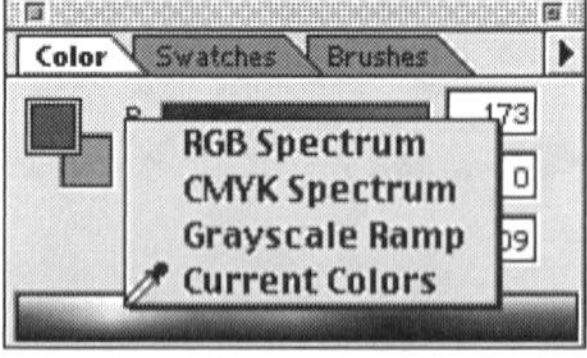

Show or Hide the Swatches Palette

Menu: Window→Show/Hide Swatches

Both: F6

F6 shows or hides the Color palette. Also use it to show or hide the Swatches palette. To show Swatches if the Color palette is not open, press F6, and then click the Swatches tab. To hide both the Swatches and the Color palettes, press the F6 key until they both disappear.

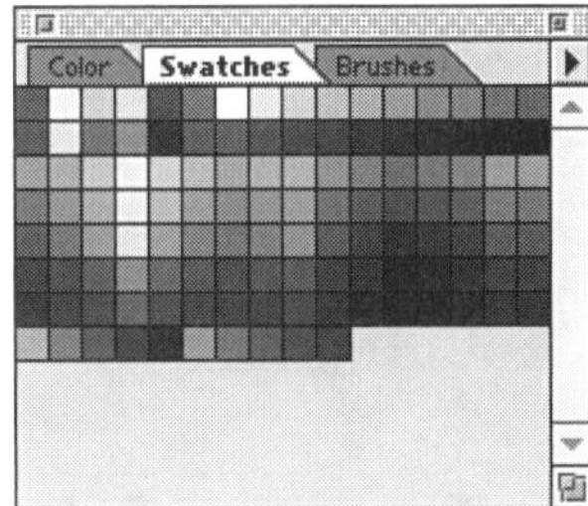

Add Foreground Color as a New Swatch

Mouse: Click on an empty slot in the Swatches palette

Look for the cursor to change into a bucket icon.

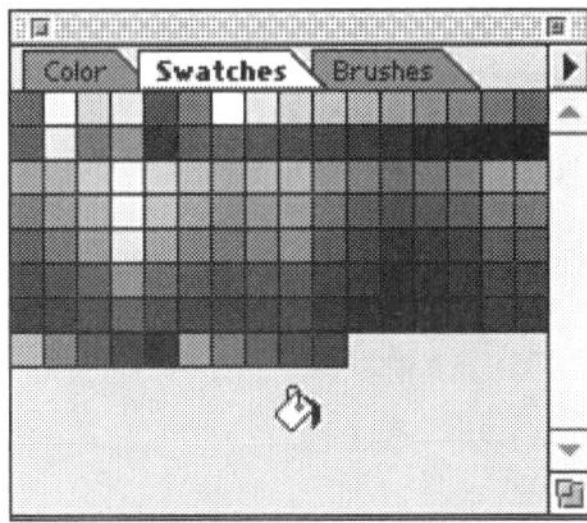

Delete a Swatch

Mac: Cmd-Click on a swatch

Win: Ctrl+Click on a swatch

Look for the cursor to change into a scissors icon.

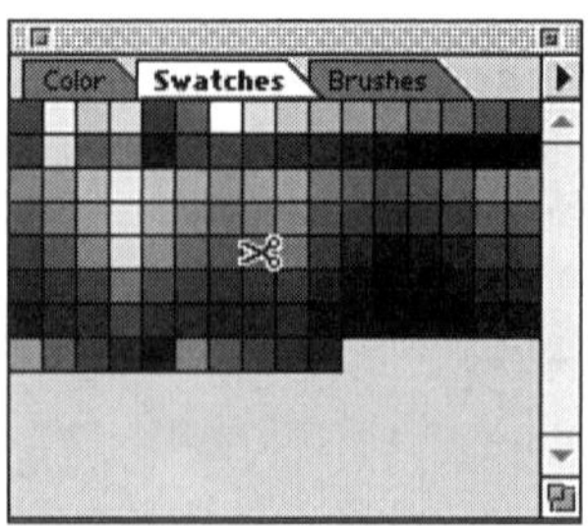

Insert Foreground Color as a New Swatch

Mac: Option-Shift-Click in the palette

Win: Alt+Shift+Click in the palette

This inserts a swatch of the current foreground color and shifts the rest of the swatches in the palette to the right.

Replace a Swatch with the Foreground Color

Mouse: Shift+Click on a swatch

Choose a Swatch for the Foreground Color

Mouse: Click on a swatch

Choose a Swatch for the Background Color

Mac: Option-Click on a swatch

Win: Alt+Click on a swatch

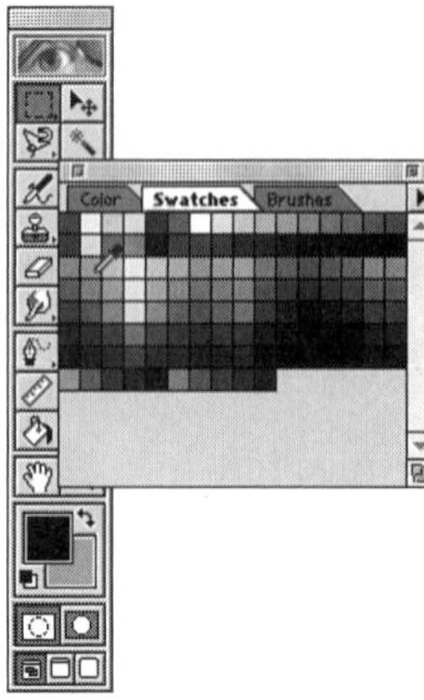

Show or Hide the Brushes Palette

Menu: Window→Show/Hide Brushes

Both: F5

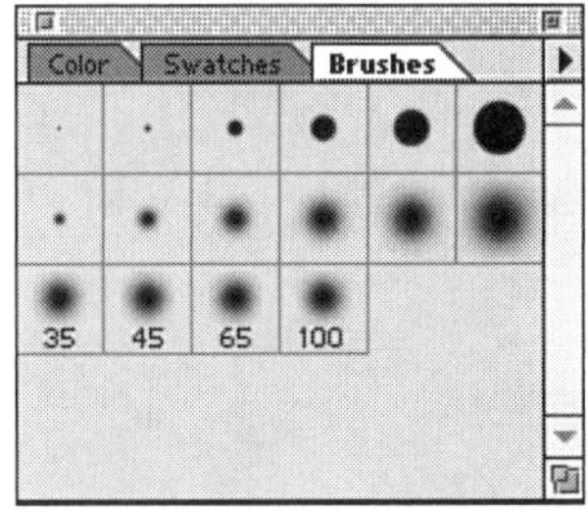

Show or Hide the Layers Palette

Menu: Window→Show/Hide Layers

Both: F7

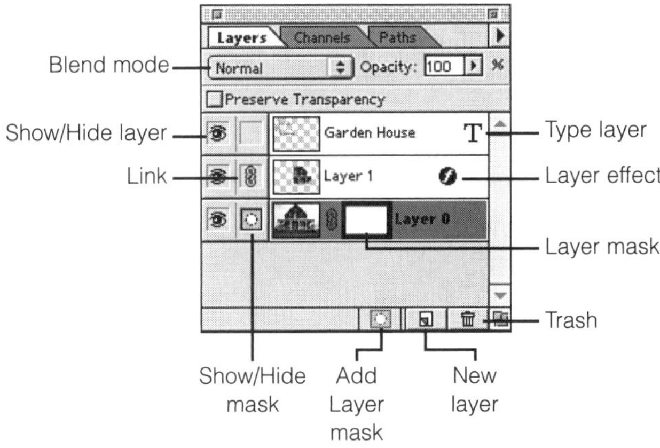

Show or Hide the Channels Palette

Menu: Window→Show/Hide Channels

Both: F7

F7 shows or hides the Layers palette. Also use it to show or hide the Channels palette. To show Channels if the Layers palette is not open, press F7, and then click the Channels tab. To hide both the Channels and the Layers palettes, press the F7 key until they both disappear.

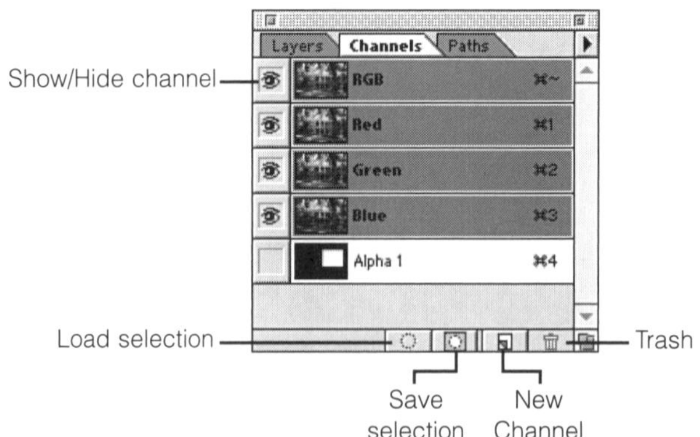

Show or Hide the Paths Palette

Menu: Window→Show/Hide Paths

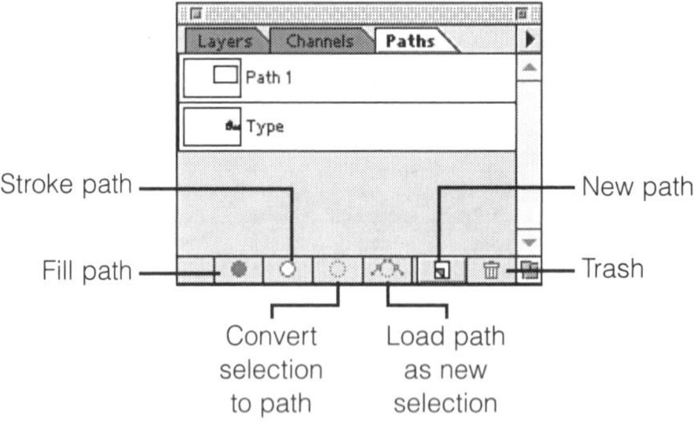

Show or Hide the History Palette

VERSION 5.0

Menu: Window→Show/Hide History

Both: F9

F9 shows or hides the Actions palette. Also use it to show or hide the History palette. To show History if the Actions palette is not open, press F9, and then click the History tab. To hide both the History and the Actions palettes, press the F9 key until they both disappear.

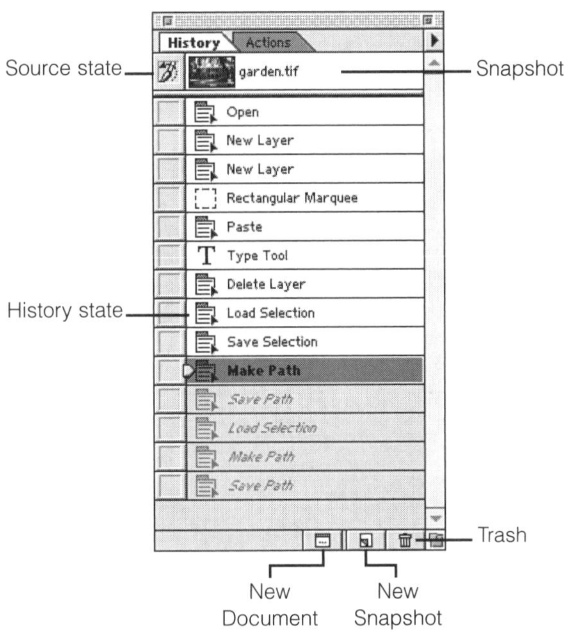

Step Backward (Multiple Undo)

VERSION 5.0

Menu: History→Step Backward

Mac: Cmd-Option-Z

Win: Ctrl+Alt+Z

Step Forward (Multiple Redo)

VERSION 5.0

Menu: History→Step Forward

Mac: Cmd-Shift-Z

Win: Ctrl+Shift+Z

Duplicate the History State (Other Than Current)

VERSION 5.0

Mac: Option-Click on state

Win: Alt+Click on state

Create a New Snapshot

VERSION 5.0

Mouse: Click the New Snapshot button

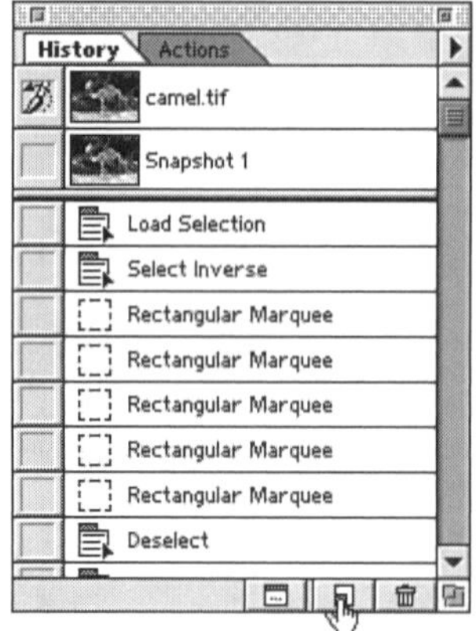

Create a New Document from the Target Snapshot

VERSION 5.0

Mouse: Click the New Document button

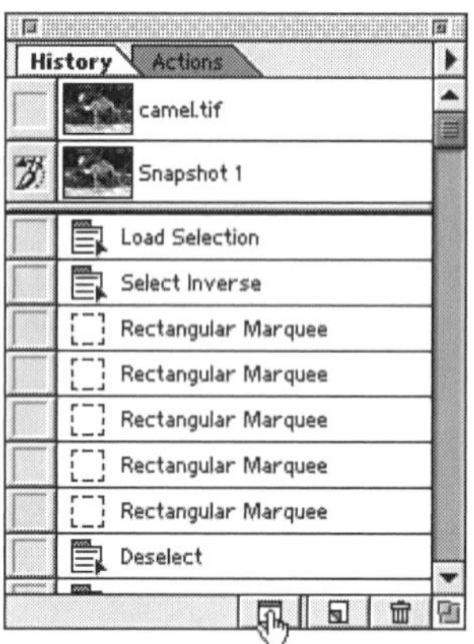

Show or Hide the Actions Palette

Menu: Window→Show/Hide Actions

Both: F9

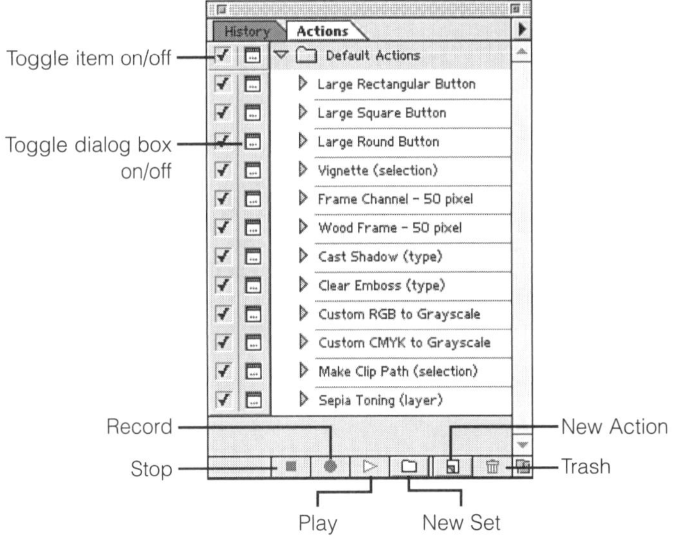

Steal the Attributes of an Open Document

Menu: Window→choose the document from the list

Here is another one of those deeply buried, not obvious, and undocumented shortcuts that make you say, "Doh! I wish I knew that years ago!" When you are compositing images together, it is often useful to make the canvas sizes of all the documents you are using the same. There are three different places you can take advantage of this trick: the New dialog box, the Image Size dialog box, and the Canvas Size dialog box. When in any of these three places, you may have never noticed that most of the menus are grayed out and unavailable. However, the Window menu is available. If you choose any open document listed in the Window menu, Photoshop automatically changes the attributes of the New, Image Size, and Canvas Size dialog boxes to match the open document.

Tools

Tool Shortcuts

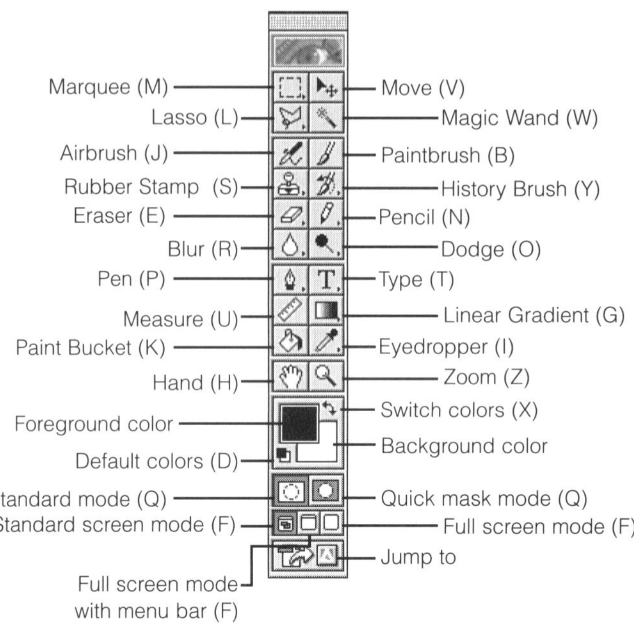

Cycle Through the Available Tools in a Tool Slot

VERSION 5.0

Mac: Option-Click on tool slot

Win: Alt+Click on tool slot

If you use the mouse to switch from tool to tool rather than using the keystroke assigned to each tool, you can avoid using the tool slot flyouts to switch to a tool that you can't see by (Option) [Alt] clicking on the tool slot. Keep clicking on the tool slot until you switch to the tool you want.

Crop Tool

VERSION 5.0

Both: C

Cycle Through Marquee Tools

VERSION 5.0

Both: Shift+M

This toggles you back and forth between the Rectangular Marquee tool and the Elliptical Marquee tool.

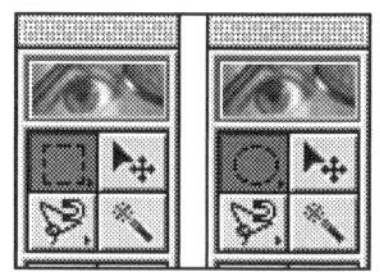

Toggle to the Move Tool

Mac: Cmd

Win: Ctrl

This allows you to temporarily switch to the Move tool while any other tool is selected.

Move the Selection Marquee 1 Pixel

Both: Arrow keys

Mouse: With a selection tool active, place cursor inside the selection, then press and drag

As long as a selection tool is active (Marquee, Lasso, Magic Wand), the arrow keys move just the selection marquee—not any pixels—one pixel in the direction of the arrow key you choose.

Move the Selection Marquee 10 Pixels

Both: Shift+Arrow keys

Mouse: With a selection tool active, place cursor inside the selection, then press and drag

As long as a selection tool is active (Marquee, Lasso, Magic Wand), holding down the Shift key and then using the arrow keys moves a selection marquee 10 pixels in the direction of the arrow key you choose.

Move the Selected Pixels 1 Pixel

Menu: Edit→Transform→Numeric

Both: Arrow keys

Mouse: With the Move tool active, press and drag

As long as the Move tool is active, the arrow keys move selected pixels one pixel in the direction of the arrow key you choose. If any other tool is active, hold down the (Cmd) [Ctrl] key, then use the arrow keys.

Move the Selected Pixels 10 Pixels

Menu: Edit→Transform→Numeric

Both: Shift+Arrow keys

Mouse: With the Move tool active, press and drag

As long as the Move tool is active, holding down the Shift key and then pressing the arrow keys moves selected pixels 10 pixels in the direction of the arrow key you choose. If any other tool is active, hold down the (Cmd+Shift) [Ctrl+Shift] keys, then use the arrow keys.

Select a Layer by Name

Mac: Ctrl-Click

Win: Right-click

This shortcut will display a pop-up menu that lists all the available layers directly under the cursor, as long as a layer actually has some pixels under the cursor. Simply choose the layer you want from the list. This shortcut illustrates the need for you to always name your layers something relevant rather than using the default names of Layer 1, Layer 2, and so on.

Select the Top-Most Visible Layer

Mac: Ctrl-Option-Click

Win: Alt+Right-click

This shortcut will select the top-most layer directly under the cursor.

Link with the Top-Most Visible Layer

Mac: Ctrl-Shift-Click

Win: Shift+Right-click

This shortcut will display a pop-up menu that lists all the available layers directly under the cursor. Instead of selecting a layer, the layer you choose will be linked with the current active layer.

Switch to the Polygonal Lasso Tool

VERSION 5.0

Mac: Option-Click

Win: Alt+Click

Draw Using the Polygonal Lasso Tool

Mac: Option-Click and drag

Win: Alt+Click and drag

This shortcut allows you to temporarily switch to the Polygonal Lasso tool while using the regular Lasso tool.

Cycle Through Lasso Tools

VERSION 5.0

Both: Shift+L

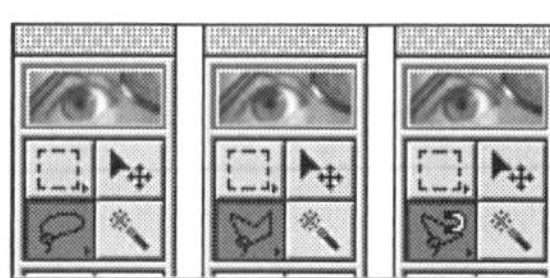

Switch to the Lasso Tool

VERSION 5.0

Mac: Option-Drag

Win: Alt+Drag

Draw Using the Lasso Tool

Mac: Option-Click and drag

Win: Alt+Click and drag

This shortcut allows you to temporarily switch to the Lasso tool while using the Polygonal Lasso tool.

Cycle Through Rubber Stamp Tools

VERSION 5.0

Both: Shift+S

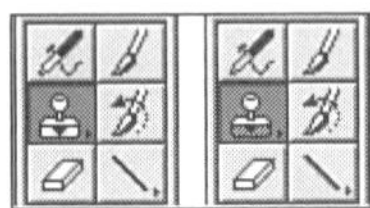

Specify the Clone Source

Mac: Option-Click

Win: Alt+Click

Cycle Through History Brush Tools

VERSION 5.5

Both: Shift+Y

Toggle Between History Brush and Art History Brush Tools

VERSION 5.5

Both: Shift+Y

Clear History Permanently

VERSION 5.0

Mac: Option-Clear History

Win: Alt+Clear History

This is not undoable!

Cycle Through Eraser Tools

VERSION 5.5

Both: Shift+E

This toggles you back and forth between the Eraser, Background Eraser, and the Magic Eraser tools. Note: There is no Background Eraser in ImageReady.

Cycle Through Eraser Tools (in the Options Palette)

VERSION 5.0

Both: Shift+E

This cycles the Eraser tool through the four painting mode options: Paintbrush, Airbrush, Pencil, and Block. In version 4, it's just the E key. In version 5.5, this functionality has been removed as Shift+E will cycle through the Eraser, Background, and Magic Eraser tools. To cycle through the mode options for the Eraser tool, you must do so manually from the pop-up menu in the Eraser Options palette.

Erase to History

VERSION 5.0

Mac: Option-Drag

Win: Alt+Drag

Cycle Through Pencil and Line Tools

VERSION 5.0

Both: Shift+N

Cycle Through Blur, Sharpen, and Smudge Tools

VERSION 5.0

Both: Shift+R

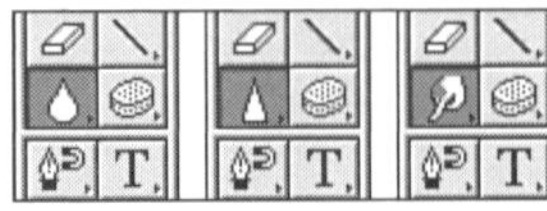

Toggle to the Blur Tool

Mac: Option

Win: Alt

Toggle to the Sharpen Tool

Mac: Option

Win: Alt

Smudge Using Foreground Color

Mac: Option

Win: Alt

Cycle Through Toning Tools

VERSION 5.0

Both: Shift+O

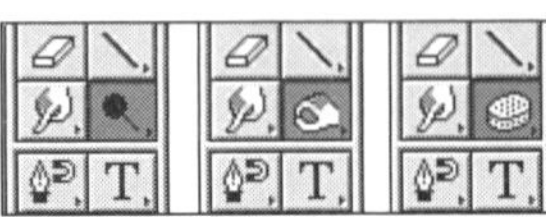

Toggle to the Dodge Tool

Mac: Option

Win: Alt

Toggle to the Burn Tool

Mac: Option

Win: Alt

Set the Dodge Tool to Affect Shadows

VERSION 5.0

Mac: Option-Shift-W

Win: Alt+Shift+W

Set the Dodge Tool to Affect Midtones

VERSION 5.0

Mac: Option-Shift-V

Win: Alt+Shift+V

Set the Dodge Tool to Affect Highlights

VERSION 5.0

Mac: Option-Shift-Z

Win: Alt+Shift+Z

Set the Burn Tool to Affect Shadows

VERSION 5.0

Mac: Option-Shift-W

Win: Alt+Shift+W

Set the Burn Tool to Affect Midtones

VERSION 5.0

Mac: Option-Shift-V

Win: Alt+Shift+V

Set the Burn Tool to Affect Highlights

VERSION 5.0

Mac: Option-Shift-Z

Win: Alt+Shift+Z

Set the Sponge Tool to Desaturate

VERSION 5.0

Mac: Option-Shift-J

Win: Alt+Shift+J

Set the Sponge Tool to Saturate

VERSION 5.0

Mac: Option-Shift-A

Win: Alt+Shift+A

Add the Anchor Point Pen Tool

VERSION 5.0

Both: + (plus)

Delete the Anchor Point Pen Tool

VERSION 5.0

Both: - (minus)

Direct the Selection Tool

VERSION 5.0

Both: A

Cycle Through Pen Tools

VERSION 5.0

Both: Shift+P

This cycles you through the Pen, Magnetic Pen, and Freeform Pen tools.

Duplicate a Path

Mac: Option-Drag path

Win: Alt+Drag path

Toggle to the Direct Selection Tool

Mac: Cmd

Win: Ctrl

You can access the Direct Selection tool temporarily while you are in any of the Pen tools by holding down the (Cmd) [Ctrl] key.

Toggle to the Convert Direction Tool

VERSION 5.0

Mac: Option

Win: Alt

Toggle Between Add and Delete Anchor Point Tools

Mac: Option

Win: Alt

This shortcut applies when the cursor is poised directly over an anchor point.

Toggle to the Group Selection Function While Using the Direct Selection Tool

Mac: Option-Click

Win: Alt+Click

Cycle Through Type Tools

VERSION 5.0

Both: Shift+T

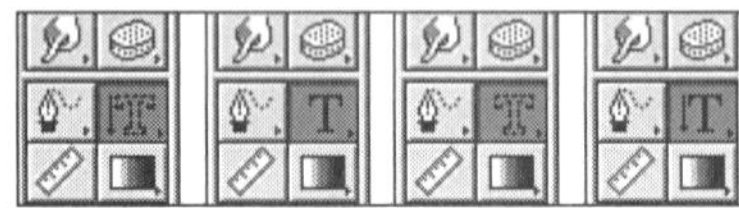

Measure Constrained to a 45-Degree Axis

VERSION 5.0

Both: Shift+Drag

Create a Protractor

VERSION 5.0

Mac: Option-Drag an end point

Win: Alt+Drag an end point

This hidden feature allows you to create a second measurement line that you can use to measure the angle of something.

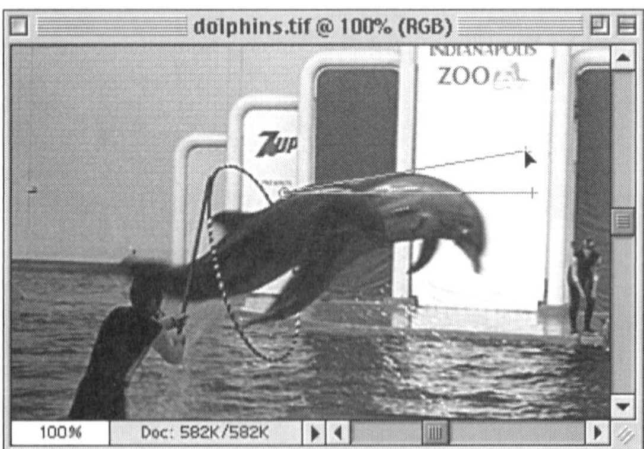

Cycle Through Gradient Tools

VERSION 5.0

Both: Shift+G

Changing the Canvas Color

Mouse: Shift+Click on the canvas with the Bucket tool

To change the canvas color from the default gray to the current foreground color, hold down the Shift key and click on the canvas with the Bucket tool. Mostly, this is a great practical joke to play on a co-worker when he mistakenly leaves Photoshop open on his machine when he goes to lunch. Then you come in and change the canvas color to toxic green. However, there is a practical reason to know about this shortcut: If you will be printing the image, it allows you to simulate what your image looks like against the color of the paper or background it will be printed on.

Cycle Through Eyedropper Tools

VERSION 5.0

Both: Shift+I

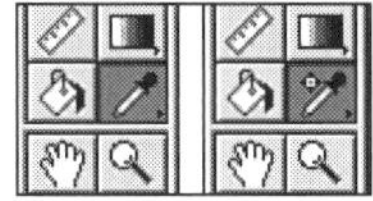

Toggle to the Eyedropper Tool

Mac: Option

Win: Alt

Hold down the specified key to temporarily switch to the Eyedropper tool so that you can choose a new foreground color. This shortcut works when using any of the following tools: Airbrush, Paintbrush, Gradient, Paint Bucket, Pencil, and Line.

Select Background Color When Using the Eyedropper Tool

Mac: Option-Click

Win: Alt+Click

Toggle to the Color Sampler Tool When Using the Eyedropper Tool

Both: Shift

Delete a Color Sampler

Mac: Option-Click

Win: Alt+Click

Delete a Color Sampler When Using the Eyedropper Tool

Mac: Option-Shift-Click on sampler

Win: Alt+Shift+Click on sampler

Toggle to the Zoom Out Tool

Mac: Option-Spacebar

Win: Alt+Spacebar

Toggle to the Zoom In Tool

Mac: Cmd-Spacebar

Win: Ctrl+Spacebar

Zoom In

Menu: View→Zoom In

Mac: Cmd-+ (plus)

Win: Ctrl++ (plus)

Mouse: Click with the Zoom (Magnifying Glass) tool

Zoom Out

Menu: View→Zoom Out

Mac: Cmd-– (minus)

Win: Ctrl+– (minus)

Both: (Option-Click) with the Zoom (Magnifying Glass) tool; [Alt+Click] with the Zoom (Magnifying Glass) tool

Exchange Foreground and Background Colors

Both: X

Mouse: Click on the curved double arrow in the Tools palette

Reset Colors Back to Defaults

Both: D

Mouse: Click on the miniature foreground/background icon in the Tools palette

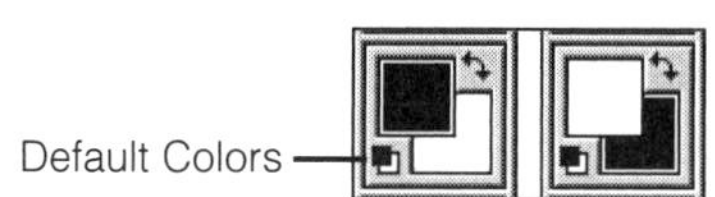

Toggle to/from Quick Mask Mode

Both: Q

Mouse: Click on the Quick Mask Mode icon in the Tools palette

Invert the Quick Mask Selection Area

Mac: Option-Click on the Quick Mask mode icon in the Tools palette

Win: Alt+Click on the Quick Mask mode icon in the Tools palette

Open the Quick Mask Mode Dialog Box

Mouse: Double-click on the Quick Mask mode icon in the Tools palette

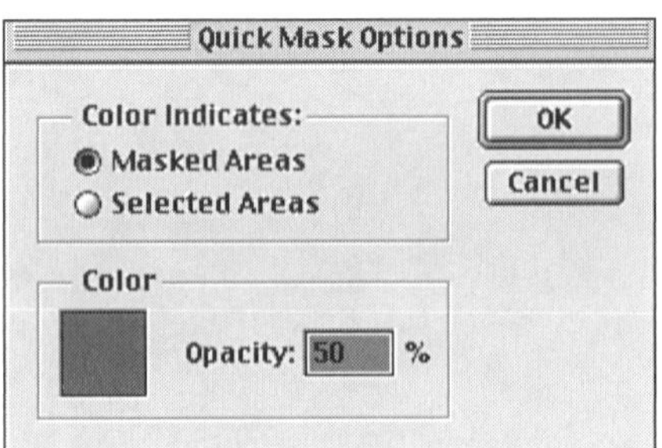

Toggle Screen Modes

Both: F

Toggle to Menus While in Full Screen Mode

VERSION 5.0

Both: Shift+F

Cropping Shortcuts

Crop Tool

Both: C

Apply Crop

Both: Enter or Return

Cancel Crop

Mac: Cmd-. (period)

Win: Ctrl+. (period)

Both: Esc

Crop Without Snapping to Edges

Mac: Cmd-Drag

Win: Ctrl+Drag

Constrain Crop to a Square

Mouse: Shift-Drag handles

Resize Crop from the Center

Mac: Option-Drag handles

Win: Alt+Drag handles

Constrain Crop from the Center

Mac: Option-Shift-Drag handles

Win: Alt+Shift+Drag handles

Rotate the Cropping Boundary

Mouse: Drag outside the cropping box

Move the Cropping Box

Mouse: Drag inside the cropping box

Resize the Cropping Box

Mouse: Drag cropping box handles

Add Canvas to an Image with the Crop Tool

Mouse: Resize cropping box beyond image area

This is another one of those cool hidden shortcuts because it isn't obvious at first. First, select the entire image area with the Crop tool. After you see the cropping box handles, you can then resize the box beyond the image area. When you apply the crop, it adds the additional canvas to the image area. To add canvas equally from the center of the image, hold down the (Option) [Alt] key while dragging a handle. Remember, you have to create a crop area first, and then you can adjust it outside the image area.

Painting Shortcuts

Select the Next Brush

Both:]

Select the Previous Brush

Both: [

Select the First Brush

Both: Shift+[

Select the Last Brush

Both: Shift+]

Create a New Brush

Both: Click in empty slot

Delete a Brush

Mac: Cmd-Click on the brush

Win: Ctrl+Click on the brush

Look for the cursor to change to a scissors icon.

Edit a Brush

Mouse: Double-click on the brush

Change Painting Tool Opacity in 1% Increments

Both: Type two numbers quickly (11=11%, 63=63%, and so on)

Change Painting Tool Opacity in 10% Increments

Both: Type a single number (1=10%, 2=20%, and so on)

Paint Constrained to Horizontal or Vertical Axis

Both: Shift+Drag

This shortcut works when using any of the following tools: Airbrush, Paintbrush, Rubber Stamp, Pattern Stamp, History Brush, Eraser, Pencil, Line, Blur, Sharpen, Smudge, Dodge, Burn, Sponge, and Gradient.

Paint or Draw in a Straight Line

Mouse: Shift+Click

This shortcut works when using any of the following tools: Airbrush, Paintbrush, Rubber Stamp, Pattern Stamp, History Brush, Eraser, Pencil, Pen, Line, Blur, Sharpen, Smudge, Dodge, Burn, Sponge, and Gradient.

Set the Brush to Threshold Paint Mode

VERSION 5.0

Mac: Option-Shift-L

Win: Alt+Shift+L

Mouse: Blend Mode pop-up menu in Layers palette

Set the Paint Bucket and Line Tools to Clear

VERSION 5.0

Mac: Option-Shift-R

Win: Alt+Shift+R

Mouse: Blend Mode pop-up menu in Layers palette

Set Tool to Next Blend Mode

VERSION 5.0

Both: Shift++ (plus)

Set Tool to Previous Blend Mode

VERSION 5.0

Both: Shift+– (minus)

Set Painting Tool to Normal Paint Mode

VERSION 5.0

Mac: Option-Shift-N

Win: Alt+Shift+N

Mouse: Blend Mode pop-up menu in Options palette

Set Painting Tool to Dissolve Paint Mode

VERSION 5.0

Mac: Option-Shift-I

Win: Alt+Shift+I

Mouse: Blend Mode pop-up menu in Layers palette

Set Painting Tool to Multiply Paint Mode

VERSION 5.0

Mac: Option-Shift-M

Win: Alt+Shift+M

Mouse: Blend Mode pop-up menu in Layers palette

Set Painting Tool to Screen Paint Mode

VERSION 5.0

Mac: Option-Shift-S

Win: Alt+Shift+S

Mouse: Blend Mode pop-up menu in Layers palette

Set Painting Tool to Overlay Paint Mode

VERSION 5.0

Mac: Option-Shift-O

Win: Alt+Shift+O

Mouse: Blend Mode pop-up menu in Layers palette

Set Painting Tool to Soft Light Paint Mode

VERSION 5.0

Mac: Option-Shift-F

Win: Alt+Shift+F

Mouse: Blend Mode pop-up menu in Layers palette

Set Painting Tool to Hard Light Paint Mode

VERSION 5.0

Mac: Option-Shift-H

Win: Alt+Shift+H

Mouse: Blend Mode pop-up menu in Layers palette

Set Painting Tool to Color Dodge Paint Mode

VERSION 5.0

Mac: Option-Shift-D

Win: Alt+Shift+D

Mouse: Blend Mode pop-up menu in Layers palette

Set Painting Tool to Color Burn Paint Mode

VERSION 5.0

Mac: Option-Shift-B

Win: Alt+Shift+B

Mouse: Blend Mode pop-up menu in Layers palette

Set Painting Tool to Darken Paint Mode

VERSION 5.0

Mac: Option-Shift-K

Win: Alt+Shift+K

Mouse: Blend Mode pop-up menu in Layers palette

Set Painting Tool to Lighten Paint Mode

VERSION 5.0

Mac: Option-Shift-G

Win: Alt+Shift+G

Mouse: Blend Mode pop-up menu in Layers palette

Set Painting Tool to Difference Paint Mode

VERSION 5.0

Mac: Option-Shift-E

Win: Alt+Shift+E

Mouse: Blend Mode pop-up menu in Layers palette

Set Painting Tool to Exclusion Paint Mode

VERSION 5.0

Mac: Option-Shift-X

Win: Alt+Shift+X

Mouse: Blend Mode pop-up menu in Layers palette

Set Painting Tool to Hue Paint Mode

VERSION 5.0

Mac: Option-Shift-U

Win: Alt+Shift+U

Mouse: Blend Mode pop-up menu in Layers palette

Set Painting Tool to Saturation Paint Mode

VERSION 5.0

Mac: Option-Shift-T

Win: Alt+Shift+T

Mouse: Blend Mode pop-up menu in Layers palette

Set Painting Tool to Color Paint Mode

VERSION 5.0

Mac: Option-Shift-C

Win: Alt+Shift+C

Mouse: Blend Mode pop-up menu in Layers palette

Set Painting Tool to Luminosity Paint Mode

VERSION 5.0

Mac: Option-Shift-Y

Win: Alt+Shift+Y

Mouse: Blend Mode pop-up menu in Layers palette

Set Painting Tool to the Next Paint mode

VERSION 5.0

Both: Shift++ (plus)

Set Painting Tool to the Previous Paint mode

VERSION 5.0

Both: Shift+– (minus)

Set Painting Tool to Behind Paint Mode

VERSION 5.0

Mac: Option-Shift-Q

Win: Alt+Shift+Q

Selection Tool Shortcuts

Constrain to a Square Selection

Mouse: Shift+Drag

This shortcut only works if you are starting a new selection. If a selection already exists, you will add to the selection instead.

Constrain to a Circle Selection

Mouse: Shift+Drag

This shortcut only works if you are starting a new selection. If a selection already exists, you will add to the selection instead.

Draw from the Center While Creating Selections

Mac: Option-Drag

Win: Alt+Drag

Normally, when creating a selection, the selection anchors itself from wherever you click, creating the selection outward from that position in a diagonal direction. With this shortcut, wherever you click becomes the center of the selection as you create it. Also, remember that this shortcut only works if you are starting a new selection. If a selection already exists, you will subtract from the selection instead.

Constrain and Draw from the Center While Creating Selections

Mac: Option-Shift-Drag

Win: Alt+Shift+Drag

Normally, when creating a selection, the selection anchors itself from wherever you click, creating the selection outward from that position in a diagonal direction. With this shortcut, wherever you click becomes the center of the selection as you create it. Also, remember that this shortcut only works if you are starting a new selection. If a selection already exists, you are left with the intersection of the selections instead.

Reposition a Selection as You Create It

Both: Spacebar

This is one of my favorite shortcuts. Sometimes you are trying to select a specific shape in an image and halfway through dragging out the selection, you realize you didn't start in the right position. Rather than starting over, just hold down the Spacebar. This allows you to drag the marquee to a different position. When you are ready to continue with the selection, just let go of the Spacebar. Remember to keep the mouse button down until you are finished making the selection.

Constrain a Selection as You Move It

Mouse: Shift+Drag

Make sure the cursor is within the selection area and that you press the mouse button down before you hold down the Shift key. If you hold down the Shift key first, you will add to the selection when you start dragging. If the cursor is outside the selected area, you will start a new selection instead of moving the existing one.

Transform a Selection

VERSION 4.0

Menu: Select→Transform Selection

Mac: Cmd-Option-T

Win: Ctrl+Alt+T

This shortcut only works in Photoshop 4. To use the Transform Selection command in Photoshop 5/5.5, you must use the menu command, or assign the menu command to an F key using Actions.

Register Items When Dragging from One Document to Another

Mouse: Shift+Drag from one document to the other

If you want the selection or layer from one document to end up in the same position in the target document you are dragging it to, make sure that they both have the same canvas size and hold down the Shift key as you drag the item to the target document. Let go of the mouse before letting go of the Shift key. Note: If the canvas sizes of the two documents are different, then holding down the Shift key places the dragged item in the center of the target document.

Duplicate a Selection

Mac: Option-Drag

Win: Alt+Drag

Add to a Selection

Mouse: Shift+Drag

This shortcut is the same when using any of the selection tools: Rectangular Marquee, Elliptical Marquee, or any of the Lasso tools. To use this shortcut with the Magic Wand tool, click instead of dragging.

Subtract from a Selection

Mac: Option-Drag

Win: Alt+Drag

This shortcut is the same when using any of the selection tools: Rectangular Marquee, Elliptical Marquee, or any of the Lasso tools. To use this shortcut with the Magic Wand tool, click instead of dragging.

Intersect with a Selection

Mac: Option-Shift-Drag

Win: Alt+Shift+Drag

This shortcut is the same when using any of the selection tools: Rectangular Marquee, Elliptical Marquee, or any of the Lasso tools. To use this shortcut with the Magic Wand tool, click instead of dragging.

Add to a Magnetic Pen Selection

VERSION 5.0

Mouse: Shift+Click then draw

This shortcut is the same when using any of the selection tools: Rectangular Marquee, Elliptical Marquee, or any of the Lasso tools.

Subtract from a Magnetic Pen Selection

VERSION 5.0

Mac: Option-Click then draw

Win: Alt+Click then draw

This shortcut is the same when using any of the selection tools: Rectangular Marquee, Elliptical Marquee, or any of the Lasso tools.

Intersect with a Magnetic Pen Selection

VERSION 5.0

Mac: Option-Shift-Click then draw

Win: Alt+Shift+Click then draw

This shortcut is the same when using any of the selection tools: Rectangular Marquee, Elliptical Marquee, or any of the Lasso tools.

Add a Point

VERSION 5.0

Mouse: Single-click

Delete the Last Point

VERSION 5.0

Both: Delete

Close the Selection

VERSION 5.0

Both: Double-click or Enter

Close the Selection at the Starting Point

VERSION 5.0

Mouse: Click on the starting point

Close the Selection Using a Straight-Line Segment

VERSION 5.0

Mac: Option-Double-click

Win: Alt+Double-click

Cancel an Operation

VERSION 5.0

Mac: Cmd-. (period)

Win: Ctrl+. (period)

Both: Escape

Increase Magnetic Lasso Width

VERSION 5.0

Both:]

Decrease Magnetic Lasso Width

VERSION 5.0

Both: [

Navigation

Navigation Shortcuts

Open Help

Menu: Help→Help Topics

Mac: Help key

Win: F1

Pan the Image

Both: Spacebar+Drag

Mouse: Press and drag with the Hand tool

Move View to New Area of Image

Both: Click in the preview area

Create New View in Navigator Palette

Mac: Cmd-Drag in the preview area

Win: Ctrl+Drag in the preview area

Change View % and Keep Focus in the View % Edit Field

Both: Shift+Return

Start-Up Tricks

VERSION 4.0

VERSION 5.5

Mac: Hold down Cmd-Option when launching Photoshop

Win: Hold down Ctrl+Alt when launching Photoshop

Not many people know these two tricks. If you hold down these two keys when you launch Photoshop, you will reveal two secret dialog boxes. The first dialog box allows you to specify which Plug-ins folder you want to use for this Photoshop session. You can arrange your plug-ins into different folders, and then only use a certain set. For instance, maybe you are going to use Photoshop for the next 3 hours to do color correction and you don't need the 112 special effects plug-ins you have installed. Throw all your production plug-ins into a separate folder and then choose that folder on start-up. This saves Photoshop from wasting RAM on plug-ins you don't need to use at that time. After you've located and selected the folder you want, hold down the modifier keys again and another dialog box appears.

The second dialog box allows you to choose which volume you want to use as the scratch disk. This is handy because if you know that you want to change it from the last time you used Photoshop, this allows you to make the change when you start up. If you don't know about this shortcut, you have to open Photoshop, make the scratch disk change in the Preferences dialog box, and then quit and restart Photoshop for it to take effect.

Note: The scratch disk trick only works in version 4 and 5.5. It does not work in version 5 and, in fact, will cause Photoshop to crash. Doh!

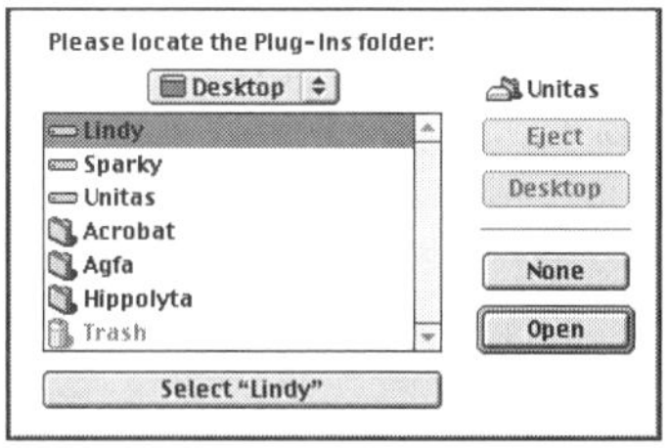

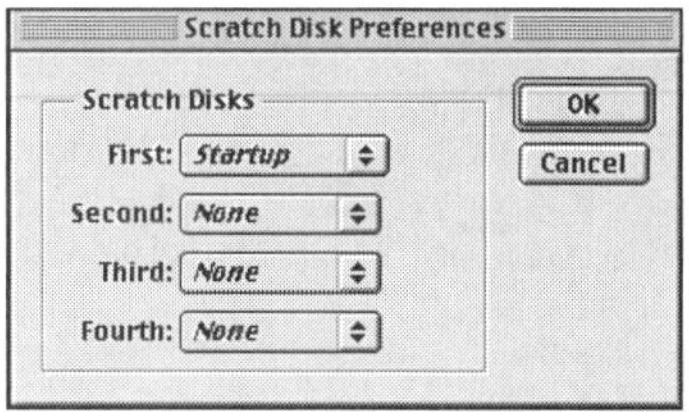

Zoom Commands

Toggle to the Zoom In Tool

Mac: Cmd-Spacebar

Win: Ctrl+Spacebar

Toggle to the Zoom In Tool

Mac: Cmd

Win: Ctrl

This shortcut is only available when the Hand tool is the active tool—if you have either clicked on the Hand tool or typed "H".

Toggle to the Zoom Out Tool

Mac: Option-Spacebar

Win: Alt+Spacebar

Toggle to the Zoom Out Tool

Mac: Option

Win: Alt

This shortcut is only available when the Hand tool is the active tool—if you have either clicked on the Hand tool or typed "H".

Zoom In

Menu: View→Zoom In

Mac: Cmd-+ (plus)

Win: Ctrl++ (plus)

Mouse: Click with the Zoom (Magnifying Glass) tool

Zoom Out

Menu: View→Zoom Out

Mac: Cmd-– (minus)

Win: Ctrl+– (minus)

Mouse: (Option+Click) [Alt+Click] with the Zoom (Magnifying Glass) tool

Zoom to 100%

Menu: View→Fit on Screen

Mac: Cmd-Option-0

Win: Ctrl+Alt+0

Mouse: Double-click on Zoom tool

Zoom to Fit Onscreen

Menu: View→Actual Pixels

Mac: Cmd-0

Win: Ctrl+0

Mouse: Double-click on Hand tool

This shortcut enlarges the window to fill as much space as the palettes leave it. Bonus tip: If you want to use the whole screen, and don't mind if the image falls behind the palettes, hide the palettes by pressing the Tab key before using this shortcut.

Zoom In Without Changing the Window Size

Mac: Cmd-Option-+ (plus)

Win: Ctrl+Alt++ (plus)

Zoom Out Without Changing the Window Size

Mac: Cmd-Option-– (minus)

Win: Ctrl+Alt+– (minus)

Scrolling Shortcuts

Scroll Viewable Area of Image

Both: Drag view proxy

Scroll Up One Full Screen

Both: Page Up

Scroll Down One Full Screen

Both: Page Down

Scroll Up 10 Pixels

Both: Shift+Page Up

Scroll Down 10 Pixels

Both: Shift+Page Down

Scroll Left One Full Screen

VERSION 5.0

Mac: Cmd-Page Up

Win: Ctrl+Page Up

Scroll Right One Full Screen

VERSION 5.0

Mac: Cmd-Page Down

Win: Ctrl+Page Down

Scroll Right 10 Pixels

VERSION 5.0

Mac: Cmd-Shift-Page Down

Win: Ctrl+Shift+Page Down

Scroll Left 10 Pixels

VERSION 5.0

Mac: Cmd-Shift-Page Up

Win: Ctrl+Shift+Page Up

Scroll to Upper-Left Corner of Image Window

Both: Home key

Power Tip: Spotting

When you want to remove dust and spots from an image, these keyboard shortcuts come in handy. Zoom up to the view you want to be in, usually 100%, and then press the Home key to begin in the upper-left corner of the image window. Then use the appropriate shortcuts to scroll down a screen at time until you get to the bottom. After you get to the bottom, use the appropriate shortcut to scroll over one screen to the right, and then start scrolling up one screen at a time. Repeat this process until you end up in the lower-right corner of the image window. The advantage of using this method is that you are guaranteed not to miss any pixels in the image. Look at the Navigator palette to see where you are in the image.

Scroll to Lower-Right Corner of Image Window

Both: End key

Dialog Boxes

Dialog Box Shortcuts

Increase Numeric Entry Values by 1

Both: Up Arrow

This works with most dialog boxes, and sometimes edits the values by .1 rather than 1 if the values allow decimal increments (for example, Feather).

Increase Numeric Entry Values by 10

Both: Shift+Up Arrow

This works with most dialog boxes, and sometimes edits the values by 1 rather than 10 if the values allow decimal increments (for example, Feather).

Decrease Numeric Entry Values by 1

Both: Down Arrow

This works with most dialog boxes, and sometimes edits the values by .1 rather than 1 if the values allow decimal increments (for example, Feather).

Decrease Numeric Entry Values by 10

Both: Shift+Down Arrow

This works with most dialog boxes, and sometimes edits the values by 1 rather than 10 if the values allow decimal increments (for example, Feather).

Cancel a Pop-Up Slider

VERSION 5.0

Both: Esc

Apply an Edit to a Pop-Up Slider

VERSION 5.0

Both: Return or Enter

Toggle to Previous Setting While Editing in a Pop-Up Slider

VERSION 5.0

Mac: Press Option while holding the mouse button down outside of a slider rectangle

Win: Press Alt while holding the mouse button down outside of a slider rectangle

Cancel Any Dialog Box

Mac: Cmd-. (period)

Win: Ctrl+. (period)

Both: Esc

Activate Any Button in an Alert Dialog Box

Both: Type the first letter of the button (for example, D = Don't Save)

Reset All Settings in a Dialog Box Without Exiting

Mac: Hold down Option to change the Cancel button to a Reset button

Win: Hold down Alt to change the Cancel button to a Reset button

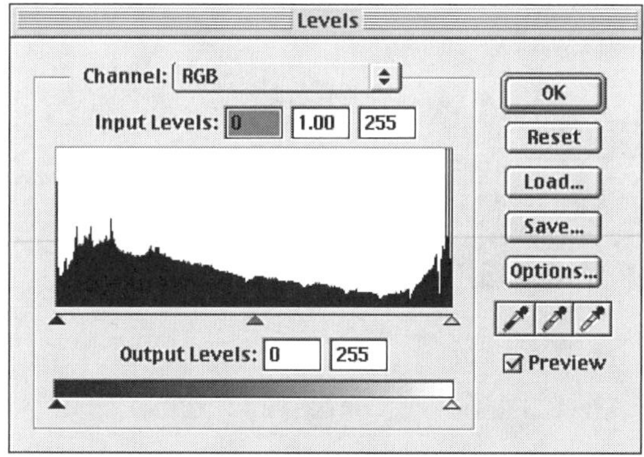

Pan Image While in a Dialog Box

Both: Spacebar+Drag

Zoom In While in a Dialog Box

Mac: Cmd-Click or Drag or Cmd-+ (plus)

Win: Ctrl+Click or Drag or Ctrl++ (plus)

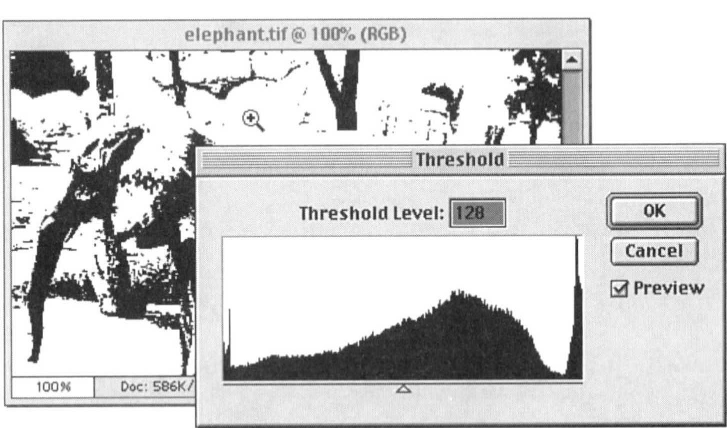

Zoom Out While in a Dialog Box

Mac: Option-Click or Drag or Cmd-– (minus)

Win: Alt+Click or Drag or Ctrl+– (minus)

The **File** Menu

File Commands

New

Menu: File→New

Mac: Cmd-N

Win: Ctrl+N

New with Last Used Settings

VERSION 5.0

Mac: Cmd-Option-N

Win: Ctrl+Alt+N

Sometimes you may notice that when you create a new document, it seems like Photoshop is just making numbers up for the dimensions (and randomly choosing the mode as well). Don't worry, there is nothing random going on here; Photoshop automatically enters in the attributes of any selection you may have copied to the Clipboard. (This in and of itself is a cool timesaver.) Use this shortcut if you want to bypass this behavior and force Photoshop to use the values of the last document you actually created.

Open

Menu: File→Open

Mac: Cmd-O

Win: Ctrl+O

Open As

Mac: Cmd-Option-O

Win: Ctrl+Alt+O

Close

Menu: File→Close

Mac: Cmd-W

Win: Ctrl+W

Save

Menu: File→Save

Mac: Cmd-S

Win: Ctrl+S

Save As

Menu: File→Save As

Mac: Cmd-Shift-S

Win: Ctrl+Shift+S

Save a Copy

Menu: File→Save a Copy

Mac: Cmd-Option-S

Win: Ctrl+Alt+S

Save for Web

VERSION 5.5

Menu: File→Save for Web

Mac: Cmd-Option-Shift-S

Win: Ctrl+Alt+Shift+S

Revert

Menu: File→Revert

Both: F12

Page Setup

Menu: File→Page Setup

Mac: Cmd-Shift-P

Win: Ctrl+Shift+P

Print

Menu: File→Print

Mac: Cmd-P

Win: Ctrl+P

Jump To [Adobe ImageReady 2.0]

VERSION 5.5

Menu: File→Jump To→Adobe ImageReady 2.0

Mac: Cmd-Shift-M

Win: Ctrl+Shift+M

Quit

Menu: File→Quit

Mac: Cmd-Q

Win: Ctrl+Q

Find

Mac: Cmd-F

Win: Ctrl+F

Both: Click the Find button in the Open dialog box

Can't find the image you are looking for? Don't remember what folder it is in? Don't sweat it. Make Photoshop do the work for you. Click the Find button or use the shortcut, type in the name or partial name of the file you are looking for, and have Photoshop find it. Photoshop displays the first occurrence of the name it finds for you. If that is not the correct file, use the Find Again command (Cmd-G) [Ctrl+G] until you find the file you are looking for. Note: You may not want to use this shortcut if you are hooked up to a network, because it can get extremely slow.

Note: This shortcut may conflict with third-party utilities that launch their own find commands.

Steal the Attributes of an Open Document

Menu: Window → choose the document from the list

Here is another one of those deeply buried, not obvious, undocumented shortcuts that make you say, "Doh! I wish I'd known that years ago!" When you are compositing images together, it is often useful to make the canvas sizes of all the documents you are using the same. There are three different places you can take advantage of this trick—the New dialog box, the Image Size dialog box, and the Canvas Size dialog box. When in any of these three places, you may have never noticed that most of the menus are greyed out and unavailable. However, the Window menu is available. If you choose any open document listed in the Window menu, Photoshop will automatically change the attributes of the New, Image Size, and Canvas Size dialog boxes to match the open document.

Preferences

Toggle Precise Cursors

Menu: File→Preferences→Display & Cursors

Both: Caps Lock

Precise Cursors changes the display of the current tool into a cross-hair target. The Caps Lock key allows you to toggle this setting, regardless of the Display & Cursors setting in the Preferences dialog box.

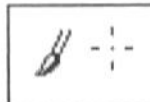

Preferences

Menu: File→Preferences

Mac: Cmd-K

Win: Ctrl+K

Reopen the Last Option Panel Used in Preferences

Menu: File→Preferences

Mac: Cmd-Option-K

Win: Ctrl+Alt+K

Open the General Panel While in the Preferences Dialog Box

Menu: File→Preferences→General

Mac: Cmd-1

Win: Ctrl+1

Open the Saving Files Panel While in the Preferences Dialog Box

Menu: File→Preferences→Saving Files

Mac: Cmd-2

Win: Ctrl+2

Open the Display & Cursors Panel While in the Preferences Dialog Box

Menu: File→Preferences→Display & Cursors

Mac: Cmd-3

Win: Ctrl+3

Open the Transparency & Gamut Panel While in the Preferences Dialog Box

Menu: File→Preferences→Transparency & Gamut

Mac: Cmd-4

Win: Ctrl+4

Open the Units & Rulers Panel While in the Preferences Dialog Box

Menu: File→Preferences→Units & Rulers

Mac: Cmd-5

Win: Ctrl+5

Open the Guides & Grid Panel While in the Preferences Dialog Box

Menu: File→Preferences→Guides & Grid

Mac: Cmd-6

Win: Ctrl+6

Open the Plug-Ins & Scratch Disks Panel While in the Preferences Dialog Box

Menu: File→Preferences→Plug-Ins & Scratch Disks

Mac: Cmd-7

Win: Ctrl+7

Open the Image Cache Panel While in the Preferences Dialog Box

Menu: File→Preferences→Image Cache

Mac: Cmd-8

Win: Ctrl+8

Switch Plug-Ins Folder or Scratch Disk When Launching Photoshop

VERSION 4.0

VERSION 5.5

Mac: Hold down Cmd-Option when launching Photoshop

Win: Hold down Ctrl+Alt when launching Photoshop

Not many people know these two tricks. If you hold down these two keys when you launch Photoshop, you will reveal two secret dialog boxes. The first dialog box allows you to specify which Plug-ins folder you want to use for this Photoshop session. You can arrange your plug-ins into different folders, and then only use a certain set. For instance, maybe you are going to use Photoshop for the next 3 hours to do color correction and you don't need the 112 special effects plug-ins you have installed. Throw all your production plug-ins into a separate folder and then choose that folder on startup. This saves Photoshop from wasting RAM on plug-ins you don't need to use at that time. After you've located and selected the folder you want, hold down the modifier keys again and another dialog box appears.

The second dialog box allows you to choose which volume you want to use as the scratch disk. This is handy because if you know that you want to change it from the last time you used Photoshop, this allows you to make the change when you start up. If you don't know about this shortcut, you have to open Photoshop, make the scratch disk change in the Preferences dialog box, and then quit and restart Photoshop for it to take effect.

Note: The scratch disk trick only works in version 4 and 5.5. It does not work in version 5 and, in fact, will cause Photoshop to crash. Doh!

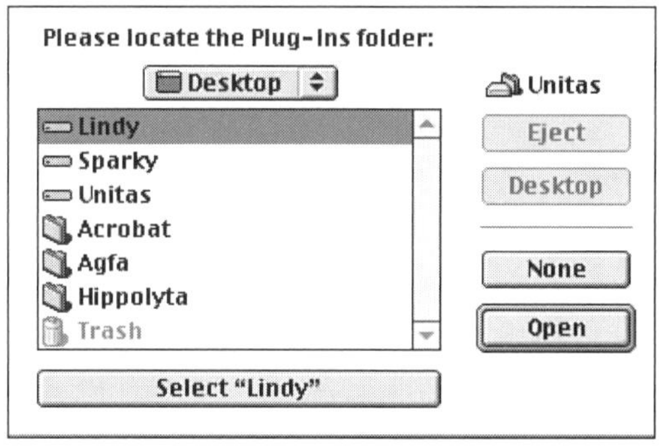

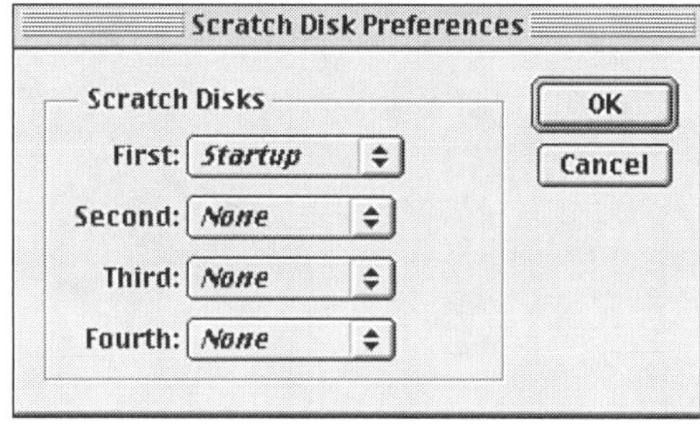

The **Edit** Menu

Edit Commands

Undo

Menu: Edit→Undo

Mac: Cmd-Z

Win: Ctrl+Z

Redo

Menu: Edit→Redo

Mac: Cmd-Z

Win: Ctrl+Z

Toggle Undo/Redo Last Step

Menu: Edit→Undo/Redo

Mac: Cmd-Z

Win: Ctrl+Z

Cut

Menu: Edit→Cut

Mac: Cmd-X

Win: Ctrl+X

Copy

Menu: Edit→Copy

Mac: Cmd-C

Win: Ctrl+C

Copy Merged

Menu: Edit→Copy Merged

Mac: Cmd-Shift-C

Win: Ctrl+Shift+C

Paste

Menu: Edit→Paste

Mac: Cmd-V

Win: Ctrl+V

Paste Into

Menu: Edit→Paste Into

Mac: Cmd-Shift-V

Win: Ctrl+Shift+V

Fill Commands

Open the Fill Dialog Box

Menu: Edit→Fill

Mac: Shift-Delete

Win: Shift+Backspace

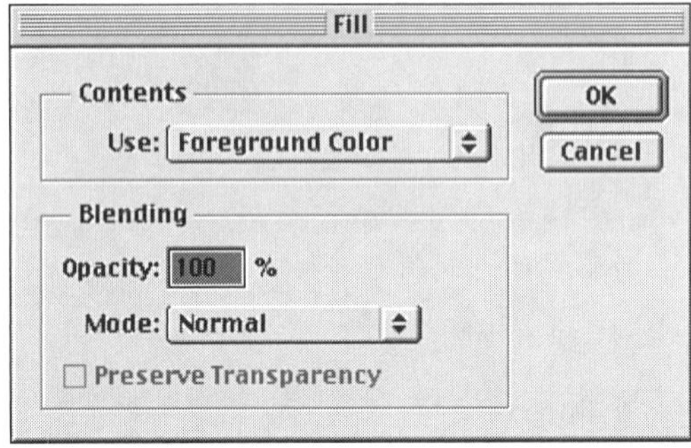

Fill with the Foreground Color

Menu: Edit→Fill

Mac: Option-Delete

Win: Alt+Backspace

Mouse: Bucket tool

This command fills the entire contents of the active layer or selection with the foreground color, unless the Preserve Transparency check box is turned on in the Layers palette.

Fill with the Foreground Color While Preserving Transparency

Menu: Edit→Fill

Mac: Option-Shift-Delete

Win: Alt+Shift+Backspace

This command only changes the color of the layer where there are actual pixels. All transparent areas are unchanged. This is an extremely efficient way to change the color of text on a Type layer. Note: Type layers always have Preserve Transparency turned on, so you CAN use the regular fill shortcuts. However, I recommend you remember this shortcut instead because it still works. That way, you only have to remember one shortcut for changing the color of type, whether it is a Type layer, or a Type layer that has been rendered.

Fill with the Background Color

Menu: Edit→Fill

Mac: Cmd-Delete

Win: Ctrl+Backspace

This command fills the entire contents of the active layer or selection with the background color.

Fill with the Background Color While Preserving Transparency

Menu: Edit→Fill

Mac: Cmd-Shift-Delete

Win: Ctrl+Shift+Backspace

This command only changes the color of the layer where there are actual pixels. All transparent areas are unchanged. This is an extremely efficient way to change the color of text on a Type layer. Note: Type layers always have Preserve Transparency turned on, so you CAN use the regular fill shortcuts. However, I recommend you remember this shortcut instead because it still works. That way, you only have to remember one shortcut for changing the color of type, whether it is a Type layer, or a Type layer that has been rendered.

Fill from History

VERSION 5.0

Menu: Edit→Fill

Mac: Cmd-Option-Delete

Win: Ctrl+Alt+Backspace

This command fills the entire contents of the active layer or selection with the active History state.

Transformation Commands

Scale Using Center Point

VERSION 5.0

Mac: Option-Drag a corner handle

Win: Alt+Drag a corner handle

Skew Using Center Point

VERSION 5.0

Mac: Cmd-Option-Drag a middle handle

Win: Ctrl+Alt+Drag a middle handle

A middle handle means any of the non-corner handles.

Snap Angle Values to 15-Degree Increments

VERSION 5.0

Both: Shift+Drag angle wheel

Apply Any Transformations

Both: Enter or Return

Cancel Any Transformations

Mac: Cmd-. (period)

Win: Ctrl+. (period)

Both: Esc

Free Transform

Menu: Edit→Free Transform

Mac: Cmd-T

Win: Ctrl+T

Transform Again

Menu: Edit→Transform→Again

Mac: Cmd-Shift-T

Win: Ctrl+Shift+T

This shortcut repeats the last transformation settings you used.

Create a Duplicate While Transforming

Mac: Cmd-Option-T

Win: Ctrl+Alt+T

Create a Duplicate While Transforming Again

Mac: Cmd-Option-Shift-T

Win: Ctrl+Alt+Shift+T

This shortcut creates a duplicate and repeats the last transformation settings you used.

Transform a Selection

VERSION 4.0

Menu: Select→Transform Selection

Mac: Cmd-Option-T

Win: Ctrl+Alt+T

This shortcut only works in Photoshop 4. To use the Transform Selection command in Photoshop 5/5.5, you must use the menu command, or assign the menu command to an F key using Actions.

Skew Using Center Point and Constrain the Axis

VERSION 5.0

Mac: Cmd-Option-Shift-Drag a middle handle

Win: Ctrl+Alt+Shift+Drag a middle handle

A middle handle means any of the non-corner handles.

Create Perspective While Using Free Transform

VERSION 5.0

Mac: Cmd-Option-Shift-Drag a corner handle

Win: Ctrl+Alt+Shift+Drag a corner handle

Distort Freely While Using Free Transform

VERSION 5.0

Mac: Cmd-Drag a handle

Win: Ctrl+Drag a handle

The **Image** Menu

Image Adjustment Commands

Color Balance

Menu: Image→Adjust→Color Balance

Mac: Cmd-B

Win: Ctrl+B

Color Balance with Last Used Settings

Mac: Cmd-Option-B

Win: Ctrl+Alt+B

Desaturate Image

Menu: Image→Adjust→Desaturate

Mac: Cmd-Shift-U

Win: Ctrl+Shift+U

Invert

Menu: Image→Adjust→Invert

Mac: Cmd-I

Win: Ctrl+I

Auto Contrast

VERSION 5.5

Menu: Image→Adjust→Auto Contrast

Mac: Cmd-Option-Shift-L

Win: Ctrl+Alt+Shift+L

See Original While in an Adjust Dialog Box

Mouse: Press on dialog box title bar with Preview off

This shortcut allows you to quickly compare the original image with the adjusted image while still in any of the Image→Adjust dialog boxes (Levels, Curves, Color Balance, Hue/Saturation, and so on). However, as you make adjustments in the dialog box, the entire monitor gets adjusted, not just the image window.

This feature only works when you have Video LUT Animation turned on in your Display & Cursors Preferences, and when the Preview check box is turned off in the Levels dialog box. Also, an additional note for Windows users: This feature only works if your video card supports Video LUT Animation.

Levels Commands

Levels

Menu: Image→Adjust→Levels

Mac: Cmd-L

Win: Ctrl+L

Levels with Last Used Settings

Mac: Cmd-Option-L

Win: Ctrl+Alt+L

Auto Levels

Menu: Image→Adjust→Auto Levels

Mac: Cmd-Shift-L

Win: Ctrl+Shift+L

Show Clipping Using Video LUT

Mac: Option-Drag sliders with Preview off

Win: Alt+Drag sliders with Preview off

This shortcut shows you which areas in your image are blowing out to complete white or black as you make tonal adjustments to the highlights and shadows of your image. This feature only works when you have Video LUT Animation turned on in your Display & Cursors Preferences, and when the Preview check box is turned off in the Levels dialog box. Also, an additional note for Windows users: This feature only works if your video card supports Video LUT Animation.

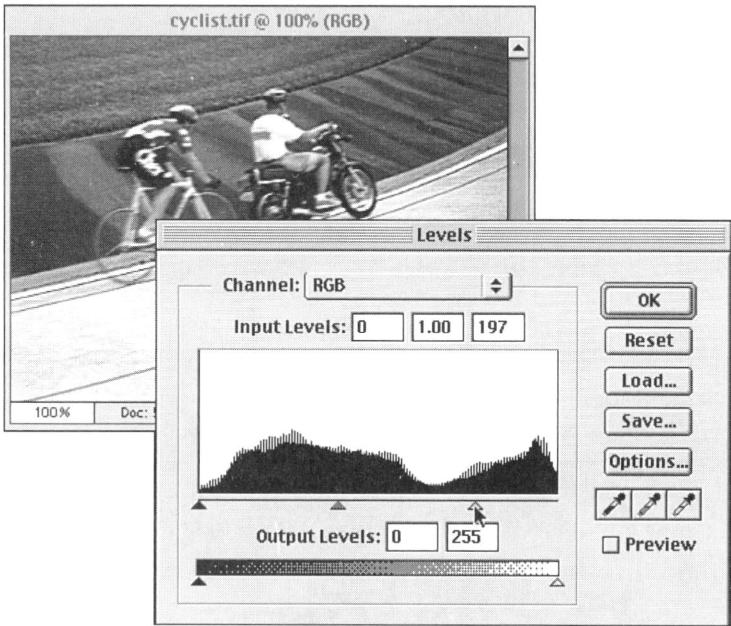

Curves Commands

Curves

Menu: Image→Adjust→Curves

Mac: Cmd-M

Win: Ctrl+M

Curves with Last Used Settings

Mac: Cmd-Option-M

Win: Ctrl+Alt+M

Pinpoint Color in Image and Place Point on Curve

Mac: Cmd-Click in image

Win: Ctrl+Click in image

If you click anywhere in an image window while the Curves dialog box is open, a hollow circle displays on the curve, which shows you where the specific color directly under the cursor falls on the curve.

If you hold down the (Cmd) [Ctrl] key, and then click in the image, a solid circle is added to the curve so that you can actually edit that specific range of color. This helps you use a visual approach to color correction.

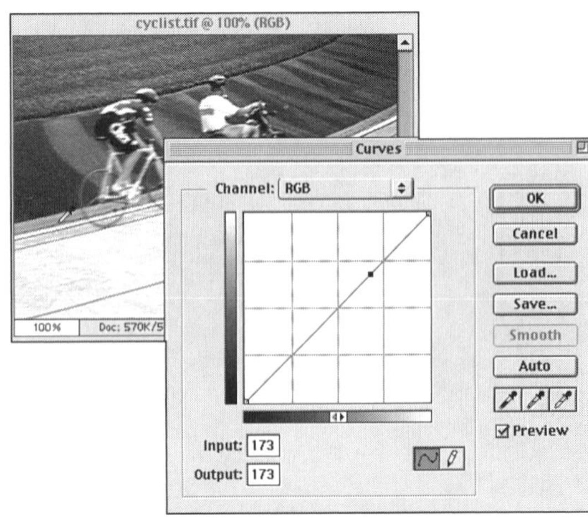

Pinpoint Color in Image and Place Points on Each Curve

Mac: Cmd-Shift-Click in image

Win: Ctrl+Shift+Click in image

If you click anywhere in an image window while the Curves dialog box is open, a hollow circle displays on the curve, which shows you where the specific color directly under the cursor falls on the curve.

If you hold down the (Cmd-Shift) [Ctrl+Shift] keys, and then click in the image, a solid circle is added to each of the individual channel's curves so that you can actually edit that specific range of color. This helps you use a visual approach to color correction.

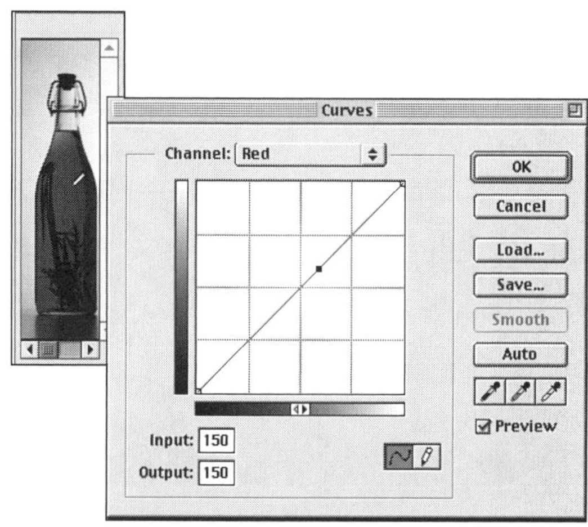

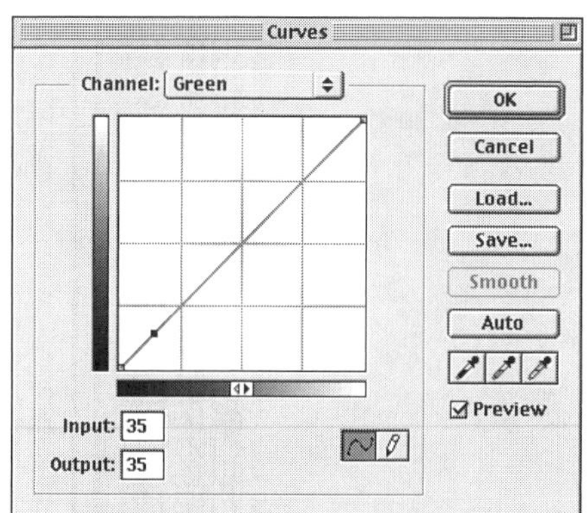

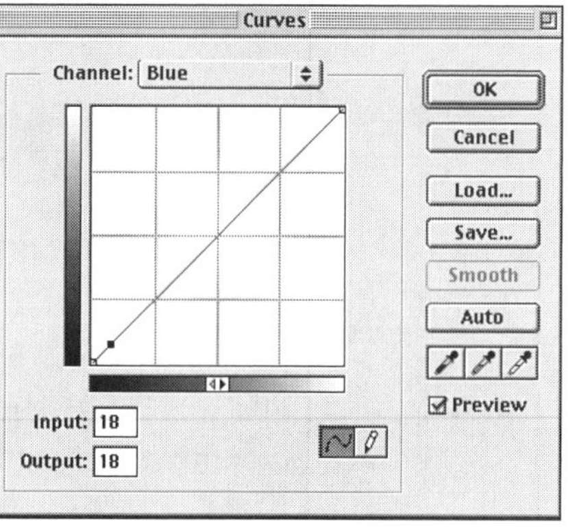

Select Next Control Point on Curve

Mac: Cmd-Tab

Win: Ctrl+Tab

If you are using Mac OS 8.5 or higher, see the following tip, "Changing the Mac OS Application Switcher," to override the system's use of the Cmd-Tab shortcut.

Select Previous Control Point on Curve

Mac: Cmd-Shift-Tab

Win: Ctrl+Shift+Tab

If you are using Mac OS 8.5 or higher, see the next tip, "Changing the Mac OS Application Switcher," to override the system's use of the Cmd-Tab shortcut.

Changing the Mac OS Application Switcher

In Mac OS 8.5 and higher, Cmd-Tab switches between open applications. To disable this so you can use Photoshop's Cmd-Tab shortcuts, follow these steps:

1. In the Finder, choose Help→Mac OS Help
2. Click "Files and Programs" in the left pane.
3. Click "Switching between open programs" in the right pane.
4. Scroll down to "Switching from one program to another" and click "Help me modify the keyboard shortcuts."
5. A dialog box might appear asking you where to find the Application Switcher. If so, navigate to the Extensions folder inside your System folder and double-click the Application Switcher.
6. Another dialog box will appear asking you if you want to use the keyboard shortcut to switch between applictions. Click No.

Select Multiple Points

Both: Shift+Click

Add Point to Curve

Both: Click in grid

Delete Point from Curve

Mac: Cmd-Click on point

Win: Ctrl+Click on point

Move Point(s)

Both: Arrow keys

Select a point or points first, and then you can move them with the arrow keys.

Move Point(s) in Multiples of 10

Both: Shift+Arrow keys

Select a point or points first, and then you can move them with the arrow keys.

Deselect All Points

Mac: Cmd-D

Win: Ctrl+D

Toggle the Size of the Grid in the Curves Dialog Box Between 10% and 25% Increments

Mac: Option-Click on grid

Win: Alt+Click on grid

Hue/Saturation Commands

Hue/Saturation

Menu: Image→Adjust→Hue/Saturation

Mac: Cmd-U

Win: Ctrl+U

Hue/Saturation with Last Used Settings

Mac: Cmd-Option-U

Win: Ctrl+Alt+U

Move Range to a New Location

VERSION 5.0

Mouse: Click in image

This only works when you're seeing the range—that is, not when you're using the Master option from the pop-up menu.

Add to Range

VERSION 5.0

Mouse: Shift+Click/Drag in image

Subtract from Range

VERSION 5.0

Mac: Option-Click/Drag in image

Win: Alt+Click/Drag in image

Edit Master

VERSION 5.0

Mac: Cmd-~ (tilde)

Win: Ctrl+~ (tilde)

Edit Individual Colors

VERSION 5.0

Mac: Cmd-[1–6]

Win: Ctrl+[1–6]

1 = Reds, 2 = Yellows, 3 = Greens, 4 = Cyans, 5 = Blues, 6 = Magentas.

Slide the Color Spectrum

VERSION 5.0

Mac: Cmd-Drag ramp

Win: Ctrl+Drag ramp

Cropping

Apply Crop

Both: Enter or Return

Cancel Crop

Mac: Cmd-. (period)

Win: Ctrl+. (period)

Both: Esc

Rotate the Cropping Boundary

Mouse: Drag outside the cropping box

Move the Cropping Box

Mouse: Drag inside the cropping box

Resize the Cropping Box

Mouse: Drag cropping box handles

Add Canvas to Image with the Crop Tool

Mouse: Resize cropping box beyond image area

This is another one of those cool hidden shortcuts because it isn't obvious at first. First, select the entire image area with the Crop tool. After you see the cropping box handles, you can then resize the box beyond the image area. When you apply the crop, it adds the additional canvas to the image area. To add canvas equally from the center of the image, hold down the (Option) [Alt] key while dragging a handle. Remember, you have to create a crop area first, and then you can adjust it outside the image area.

Constrain Crop to a Square

Both: Shift+Drag handles

Resize Crop from the Center

Mac: Option-Drag handles

Win: Alt+Drag handles

Constrain Crop from the Center

Mac: Option-Shift-Drag handles

Win: Alt+Shift+Drag handles

Crop Without Snapping to Edges

Mac: Cmd-Drag

Win: Ctrl+Drag

Extract Tool Options

Extract

VERSION 5.5

Menu: Image→Extract

Mac: Cmd-Option-X

Win: Ctrl+Alt+X

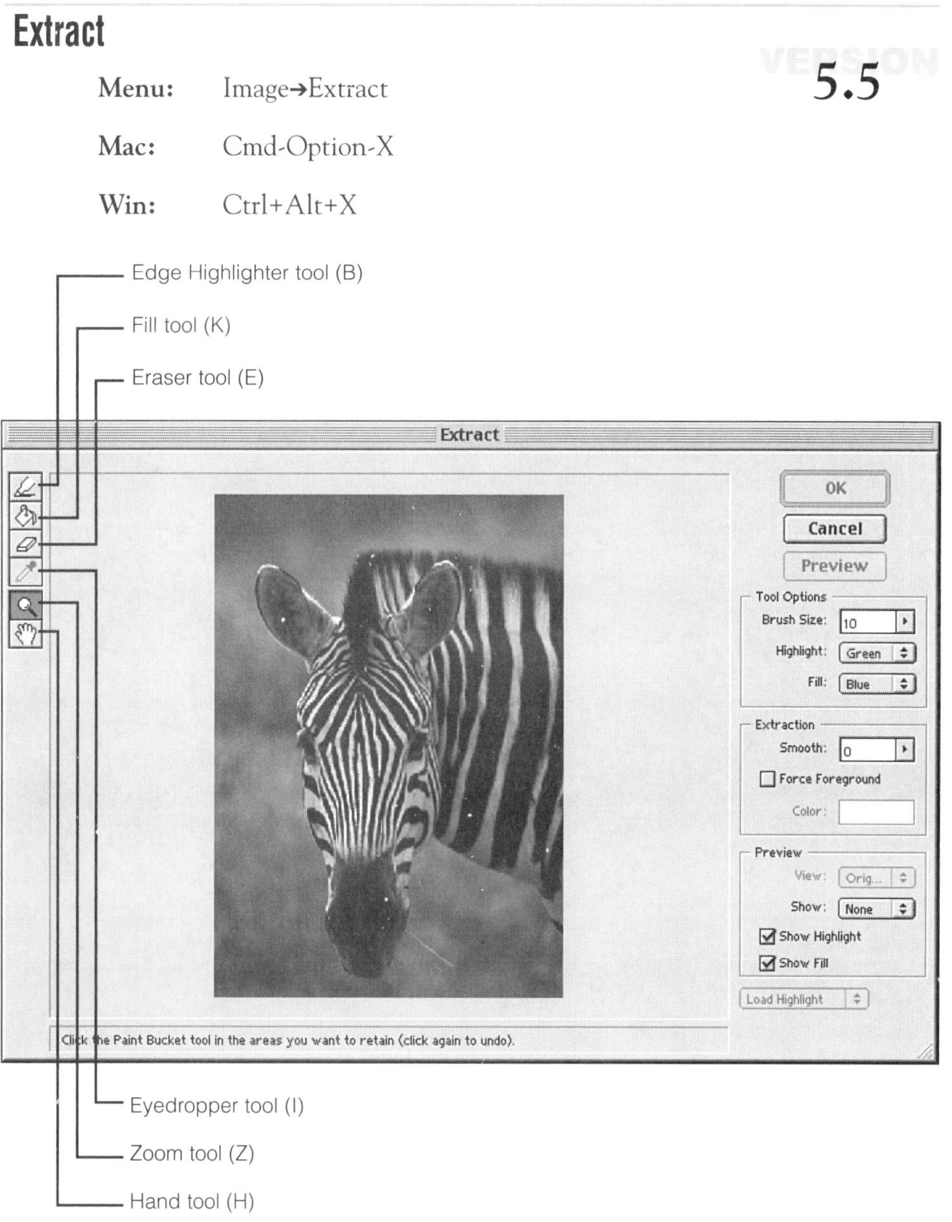

Reverse Tool Behavior

VERSION 5.5

Mac: Option

Win: Alt

For example, if you are using the Edge Highlighter tool, this shortcut switches you to the Eraser tool.

The **Layers** Menu

Creating and Deleting Layers

Create a New Layer with the New Layer Dialog Box

VERSION 5.0

Menu: Layer→New→Layer

Mac: Option-Click on New Layer icon or Cmd-Shift-N

Win: Alt+Click on New Layer icon or Ctrl+Shift+N

This method presents the New Layer dialog box, giving you a chance to name the new layer and specify other options such as opacity and blend mode as you create the layer.

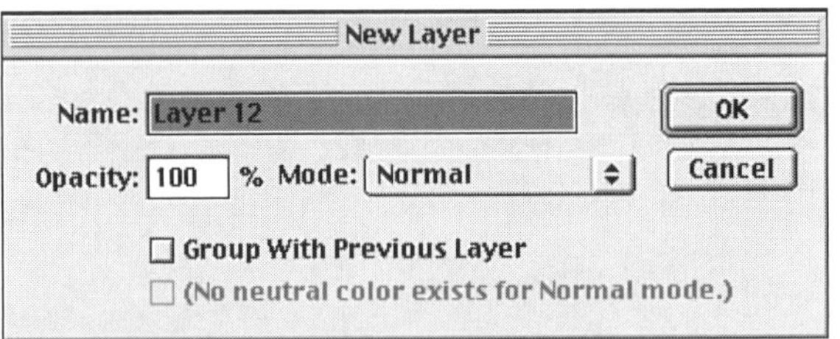

Create a New Layer and Bypass the New Layer Dialog Box

VERSION 5.0

Menu: (Option)+Layer→New→Layer; [Alt]+Layer→New→Layer

Mac: Cmd-Option-Shift-N

Win: Ctrl+Alt+Shift+N

Mouse: Click the New Layer icon

This shortcut skips the New Layer dialog box when creating a new layer. Layers are named automatically (Layer 1, Layer 2, and so on). Just hold down the specified modifier key as you choose the menu command.

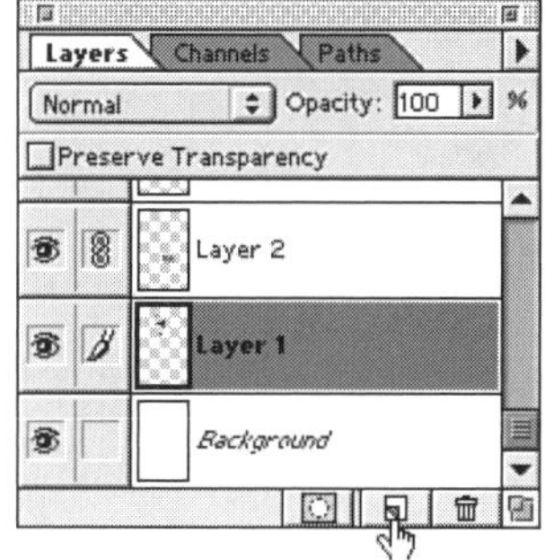

New Layer Via Copy

Menu: Layer→New→Layer Via Copy

Mac: Cmd-J

Win: Ctrl+J

New Layer Via Cut

Menu: Layer→New→Layer Via Cut

Mac: Cmd-Shift-J

Win: Ctrl+Shift+J

New Layer Via Copy with Make Layer Dialog Box

Menu: Layer→New→Layer Via Copy

Mac: Cmd-Option-J

Win: Ctrl+Alt+J

New Layer Via Cut with Make Layer Dialog Box

Menu: Layer→New→Layer Via Cut

Mac: Cmd-Option-Shift-J

Win: Ctrl+Option+Shift+J

Duplicate a Layer, Part 1

Mac: Cmd-A, Cmd-J

Win: Ctrl+A, Ctrl+J

Mouse: Drag the layer to the New Layer button

There is no single keyboard shortcut for duplicating an existing layer; however, there is a workaround. First, use the Select All command, and then use the Copy Selection Into a New Layer command. This may seem kind of silly at first—why not just use the standard method of dragging the layer's name to the New Layer button? When you drag a layer to the New Layer button while recording an Action, the layer's actual name gets included in the Action. This can create problems when you want to play the Action back sometime in the future. For instance, if you dragged a layer named "Bob" to the New Layer button, the name "Bob" is included in the Action. The next time you play the Action, if there is not a layer named "Bob" in the current file, your Action will not work.

Duplicate a Layer, Part 2

Mac: Cmd-Option-Arrow key

Win: Ctrl+Alt+Arrow key

Mouse: Drag the layer to the New Layer button

Okay, I lied. There actually is a keyboard shortcut for duplicating an existing layer. However, there's a catch, so it is only a half-lie. This shortcut also moves the duplicated layer one pixel in the direction of the arrow key that you used. So, if you plan on moving the duplicated layer anyway, this is no big deal, and is a great shortcut. However, if you need the duplicated layer to be in the exact same position as the original, then you will need to press the opposite arrow key once to get it back to the original position.

Note: If there is an active selection, this shortcut actually duplicates the selection and moves it on the target layer, not on a duplicate layer.

Create a New Adjustment Layer

Menu: Layer→New→Adjustment Layer

Mac: Cmd-Click the New Layer button

Win: Ctrl+Click the New Layer button

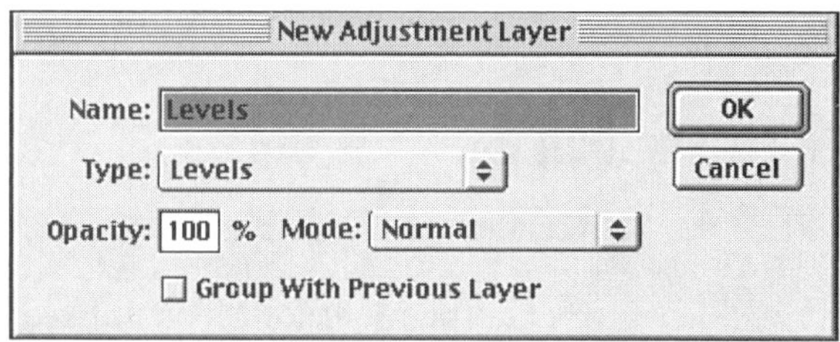

Delete a Layer

Mouse: Click the Delete Layer button

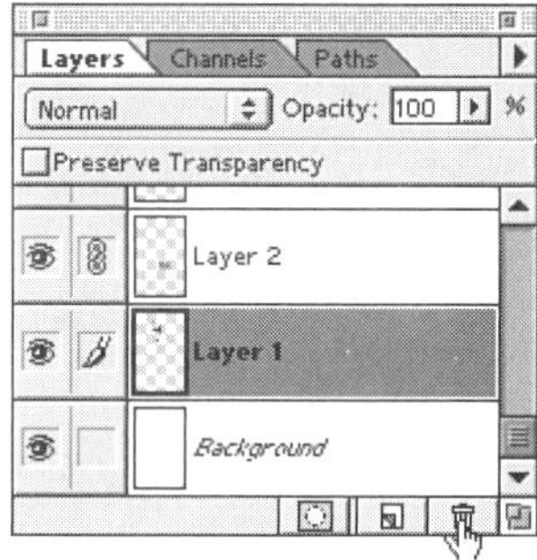

Delete a Layer and Skip the Warning Alert

Mac: Option-Click the Delete Layer button

Win: Alt+Click the Delete Layer button

Delete Multiple Layers, Part 1

Both: Merge Visible, and then click the Delete Layer button

There is no way to select multiple layers to delete them all at once. However, there is a shortcut. First, hide all the layers you want to keep, and then use the Merge Visible shortcut to merge all the layers you want to delete into a single layer. Now, simply delete this single composite layer.

Delete Multiple Layers, Part 2

Both: Use the Merged Linked command

In an odd twist, when you use the Merge or Merge Linked command with linked layers that are hidden, they get deleted! So, if there are several layers you want to get rid of, use the shortcut to hide all the layers but one, and then link all the layers you want to delete to the target layer. When you use the Merge or Merge Linked command, all the linked layers are deleted, although the target layer is kept.

Selecting and Showing Layer Commands

Show or Hide a Layer

Mouse: Click in Eye icon area

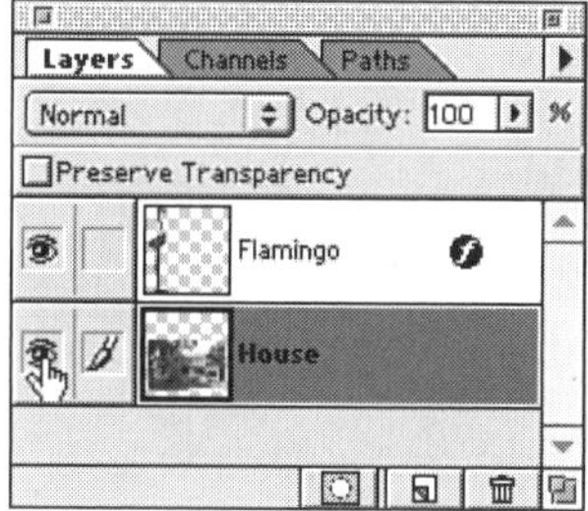

Show Just This Layer/Show All Layers

Mac: Option-Click in Eye icon area

Win: Alt+Click in Eye icon area

View and Select One Layer at a Time

Mac: Option-Click on layer name

Win: Alt+Click on layer name

This tip works when only one layer is currently visible. In other words, hide all other layers except one, and then you can use this tip to simultaneously show the next layer you select and hide the previously shown layer. Note: There is a subtle difference here when clicking on the layer name versus clicking on the eyeball area. If you click on the eyeball area instead, the previous layer stays selected as the active layer, not the layer you just clicked the eyeball for.

Show/Hide Multiple Layers

Mouse: Drag through Eye icon area

Activate Next Visible Layer (Up)

Mac: Option-]

Win: Alt+]

Activate Previous Visible Layer (Down)

Mac: Option-[

Win: Alt+[

Activate the Bottom Layer

Mac: Option-Shift-[

Win: Alt+Shift+[

Activate the Top Layer

Mac: Option-Shift-]

Win: Alt+Shift+]

Select a Layer by Name

Mac: Ctrl-Click

Win: Right-click

This shortcut displays a pop-up menu that lists all the available layers directly under the cursor, as long as a layer actually has some pixels under the cursor. Simply choose the layer you want from the list. This shortcut illustrates the need for you to always name your layers something relevant rather than using the default names of Layer 1, Layer 2, and so on.

Select the Top-Most Visible Layer

Mac: Ctrl-Option-Click

Win: Alt+Right-click

This shortcut selects the top-most layer directly under the cursor.

Layer Editing Commands

Change Layer Opacity in 1% Increments

Both: Type two numbers quickly (11=11%, 63=63%, and so on)

This shortcut only works when you have a selection or the Move tool is the active tool. Otherwise, this shortcut changes the opacity of the active Painting tool.

Change Layer Opacity in 10% Increments

Both: Type a single number (1=10%, 2=20%, and so on)

This shortcut only works when you have a selection or the Move tool is the active tool. Otherwise, this shortcut changes the opacity of the active Painting tool.

Edit Layer Options

Menu: Layer→Layer Options

Mouse: Double-click layer thumbnail or layer name

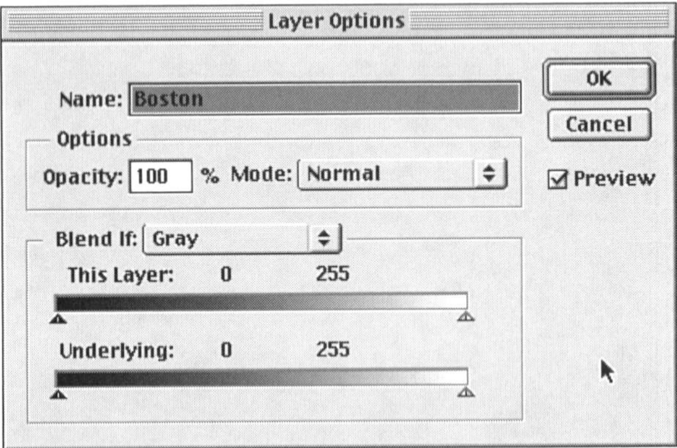

Edit Adjustment Layer Options

Menu: Layer→Adjustment Options

Mouse: Double-click Adjustment icon

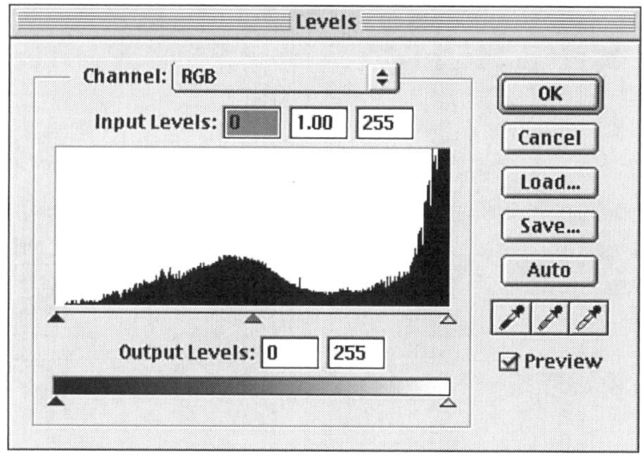

Convert a Background Layer

Mouse: Double-click on the background layer and change its name

Or, with the Move tool selected, nudge the layer up and then down by one pixel using the up- and down-arrow keys.

The background layer cannot support transparency. Use these shortcuts to convert a background layer into a layer that does support transparency. The default name is Layer 0, but you can change the name to anything you want. You also need to convert a background layer if you want to reposition it in the layer stack.

Note: If you want to add a background layer back to a file, the only choice is to use the Layer→New→Background menu command.

Moving Layers

Move Layer One Pixel

Menu: Edit→Transform→Numeric

Both: Arrow keys

Mouse: With the Move tool active, press and drag

As long as the Move tool is active, the arrow keys move a layer one pixel in the direction of the arrow key you choose. If any other tool is active, hold down the (Cmd) [Ctrl] key, and then use the arrow keys.

Move Layer 10 Pixels

Menu: Edit→Transform→Numeric

Both: Shift+Arrow keys

Mouse: With the Move tool active, press and drag

As long as the Move tool is active, holding down the Shift key and then pressing the arrow keys moves a layer 10 pixels in the direction of the arrow key you choose. If any other tool is active, hold down the (Cmd-Shift) [Ctrl+Shift] keys, and then use the arrow keys.

Move Target Layer Up

Menu: Layer→Arrange→Bring Forward

Mac: Cmd-]

Win: Ctrl+]

Move Target Layer Down

Menu: Layer→Arrange→Send Backward

Mac: Cmd-[

Win: Ctrl+[

Move Target Layer to Top

Menu: Layer→Arrange→Bring to Front

Mac: Cmd-Shift-]

Win: Ctrl+Shift+]

Move Target Layer to Bottom

Menu: Layer→Arrange→Send to Back

Mac: Cmd-Shift-[

Win: Ctrl+Shift+[

Note: If there is a background layer in the file, the target layer will stop above the background layer. To move a layer below the background layer, you must convert the background layer to a layer that supports transparency first.

Center When Dragging from One File to Another

Mouse: Shift+Drag from one document to the other

If you want the selection or layer from one document to end up in the middle of the document you are dragging it to, hold down the Shift key and drag the item to the target document. Let go of the mouse before letting go of the Shift key. Note: If the canvas sizes of the two documents are the same, holding down the Shift key places the dragged item in the target document in the same position as the original document.

Register Items When Dragging from One Document to Another

Mouse: Shift+Drag from one document to the other

If you want the selection or layer from one document to end up in the same position in the target document you are dragging it to, make sure that they both have the same canvas size and hold down the Shift key as you drag the item to the target document. Let go of the mouse before letting go of the Shift key. Note: If the canvas sizes of the two documents are different, holding down the Shift key places the dragged item in the center of the target document.

Linking and Grouping Shortcuts

Link a Layer to Current Target Layer

Mouse: Click in the Link icon area

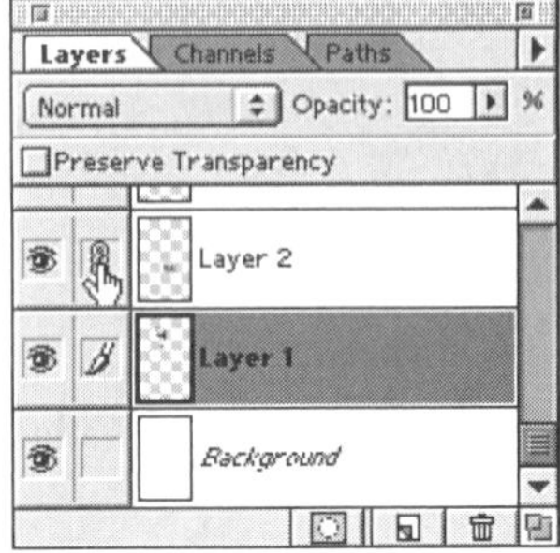

Turn On/Off Linking for Multiple Layers

Mouse: Drag in the Link icon area

Link with the Top-Most Visible Layer

Mac: Ctrl-Shift-Click

Win: Shift+Right-click

This shortcut displays a pop-up menu that lists all the available layers directly under the cursor. Instead of selecting a layer, the layer you choose will be linked with the current active layer.

Group Target Layer with Layer Below

Menu: Layer→Group with Previous

Mac: Cmd-G

Win: Ctrl+G

Ungroup Target Layer with Layer Below

Menu: Layer→Ungroup

Mac: Cmd-Shift-G

Win: Ctrl+Shift+G

Toggle Group/Ungroup with Previous Layer

Mac: Option-Click on divider between layers

Win: Alt+Click on divider between layers

Layer Merging Commands

Merge Target Layer into the Layer Below

Menu: Layer→Merge Down

Mac: Cmd-E

Win: Ctrl+E

This command merges the target layer with the layer below it, as long as the layer below the target layer is visible. The name of the layer below the target layer is the name that is kept.

Merge All Visible Layers into the Target Layer

Menu: Layer→Merge Visible

Mac: Cmd-Shift-E

Win: Ctrl+Shift+E

This command merges all visible layers into the target layer. The name of the target layer is the name that is kept.

Merge a Copy of All Visible Layers into the Target Layer

Both: (Option) [Alt]+Merge Visible

Mac: Cmd-Option-Shift-E

Win: Ctrl+Alt+Shift+E

This command merges a copy of all the visible layers into the target layer, leaving the original layers intact. However, this does change the target layer. What you might want to do instead is to create a composite copy of all visible layers into a new layer. To accomplish this, just do the obvious: Create a new layer before using this shortcut. This is a great shortcut to use when making individual frames of an animation by hand. Each frame ends up being a composite of the individual layers. After you have the individual layers set up the way you want them for a particular animation frame, create a new empty layer and use this shortcut. Modify the individual layers for the next frame and repeat the process.

Merge All Linked Layers into the Target Layer

Menu: Layer→Merge Linked

Mac: Cmd-E

Win: Ctrl+E

This command merges all the linked layers into the target layer—as long as the linked layers are visible! If any of the linked layers are hidden, they are deleted. This is actually a great tip to effectively merge the layers you want to composite and delete the layers you don't want at the same time.

Merge a Copy of the Target Layer into the Layer Below

Mac: Cmd-Option-E or Option-Layer→Merge Down

Win: Ctrl+Alt+E or Alt+Layer→Merge Down

This command merges a copy of the target layer with the layer below it, as long as the layer below the target layer is visible.

Merge a Copy of All Linked Layers into the Target Layer

Mac: Cmd-Option-E or Option-Layers→Merge Linked

Win: Ctrl+Alt+E or Alt+Layers→Merge Linked

This command merges a copy of all the visible linked layers into the target layer.

Blend Mode Shortcuts

Set Layer to Next Blend Mode

VERSION 5.0

Both: Shift++ (plus)

This shortcut only works when you have a selection or the Move tool is the active tool. Otherwise, this shortcut changes the opacity of the active Painting tool.

Set Layer to Previous Blend Mode

VERSION 5.0

Both: Shift+- (minus)

This shortcut only works when you have a selection or the Move tool is the active tool. Otherwise, this shortcut changes the opacity of the active Painting tool.

Set Layer to Normal Blend Mode

VERSION 5.0

Mac: Option-Shift-N

Win: Alt+Shift+N

Mouse: Blend Mode pop-up menu in Layers palette

This shortcut only works when you have a selection or the Move tool is the active tool. Otherwise, this shortcut changes the opacity of the active Painting tool.

Set Layer to Dissolve Blend Mode

VERSION 5.0

Mac: Option-Shift-I

Win: Alt+Shift+I

Mouse: Blend Mode pop-up menu in Layers palette

This shortcut only works when you have a selection or the Move tool is the active tool. Otherwise, this shortcut changes the opacity of the active Painting tool.

Set Layer to Multiply Blend Mode

VERSION 5.0

Mac: Option-Shift-M

Win: Alt+Shift+M

Mouse: Blend Mode pop-up menu in Layers palette

This shortcut only works when you have a selection or the Move tool is the active tool. Otherwise, this shortcut changes the opacity of the active Painting tool.

Set Layer to Screen Blend Mode

VERSION 5.0

Mac: Option-Shift-S

Win: Alt+Shift+S

Mouse: Blend Mode pop-up menu in Layers palette

This shortcut only works when you have a selection or the Move tool is the active tool. Otherwise, this shortcut changes the opacity of the active Painting tool.

Set Layer to Overlay Blend Mode

VERSION 5.0

Mac: Option-Shift-O

Win: Alt+Shift+O

Mouse: Blend Mode pop-up menu in Layers palette

This shortcut only works when you have a selection or the Move tool is the active tool. Otherwise, this shortcut changes the opacity of the active Painting tool.

Set Layer to Soft Light Blend Mode

VERSION 5.0

Mac: Option-Shift-F

Win: Alt+Shift+F

Mouse: Blend Mode pop-up menu in Layers palette

This shortcut only works when you have a selection or the Move tool is the active tool. Otherwise, this shortcut changes the opacity of the active Painting tool.

Set Layer to Hard Light Blend Mode

VERSION 5.0

Mac: Option-Shift-H

Win: Alt+Shift+H

Mouse: Blend Mode pop-up menu in Layers palette

This shortcut only works when you have a selection or the Move tool is the active tool. Otherwise, this shortcut changes the opacity of the active Painting tool.

Set Layer to Color Dodge Blend Mode

VERSION 5.0

Mac: Option-Shift-D

Win: Alt+Shift+D

Mouse: Blend Mode pop-up menu in Layers palette

This shortcut only works when you have a selection or the Move tool is the active tool. Otherwise, this shortcut changes the opacity of the active Painting tool.

Set Layer to Color Burn Blend Mode

VERSION 5.0

Mac: Option-Shift-B

Win: Alt+Shift+B

Mouse: Blend Mode pop-up menu in Layers palette

This shortcut only works when you have a selection or the Move tool is the active tool. Otherwise, this shortcut changes the opacity of the active Painting tool.

Set Layer to Darken Blend Mode

VERSION 5.0

Mac: Option-Shift-K

Win: Alt+Shift+K

Mouse: Blend Mode pop-up menu in Layers palette

This shortcut only works when you have a selection or the Move tool is the active tool. Otherwise, this shortcut changes the opacity of the active Painting tool.

Set Layer to Lighten Blend Mode

VERSION 5.0

Mac: Option-Shift-G

Win: Alt+Shift+G

Mouse: Blend Mode pop-up menu in Layers palette

This shortcut only works when you have a selection or the Move tool is the active tool. Otherwise, this shortcut changes the opacity of the active Painting tool.

Set Layer to Difference Blend Mode

VERSION 5.0

Mac: Option-Shift-E

Win: Alt+Shift+E

Mouse: Blend Mode pop-up menu in Layers palette

This shortcut only works when you have a selection or the Move tool is the active tool. Otherwise, this shortcut changes the opacity of the active Painting tool.

Set Layer to Exclusion Blend Mode

VERSION 5.0

Mac: Option-Shift-X

Win: Alt+Shift+X

Mouse: Blend Mode pop-up menu in Layers palette

This shortcut only works when you have a selection or the Move tool is the active tool. Otherwise, this shortcut changes the opacity of the active Painting tool.

Set Layer to Hue Blend Mode

VERSION 5.0

Mac: Option-Shift-U

Win: Alt+Shift+U

Mouse: Blend Mode pop-up menu in Layers palette

This shortcut only works when you have a selection or the Move tool is the active tool. Otherwise, this shortcut changes the opacity of the active Painting tool.

Set Layer to Saturation Blend Mode

VERSION 5.0

Mac: Option-Shift-T

Win: Alt+Shift+T

Mouse: Blend Mode pop-up menu in Layers palette

This shortcut only works when you have a selection or the Move tool is the active tool. Otherwise, this shortcut changes the opacity of the active Painting tool.

Set Layer to Color Blend Mode

VERSION 5.0

Mac: Option-Shift-C

Win: Alt+Shift+C

Mouse: Blend Mode pop-up menu in Layers palette

This shortcut only works when you have a selection or the Move tool is the active tool. Otherwise, this shortcut changes the opacity of the active Painting tool.

Set Layer to Luminosity Blend Mode

VERSION 5.0

Mac: Option-Shift-Y

Win: Alt+Shift+Y

Mouse: Blend Mode pop-up menu in Layers palette

This shortcut only works when you have a selection or the Move tool is the active tool. Otherwise, this shortcut changes the opacity of the active Painting tool.

Transparency Shortcuts

Toggle Preserve Transparency On and Off for Target Layer

Both: / (forward slash)

Load Layer Transparency as a Selection

Mac: Cmd-Click on layer

Win: Ctrl+Click on layer

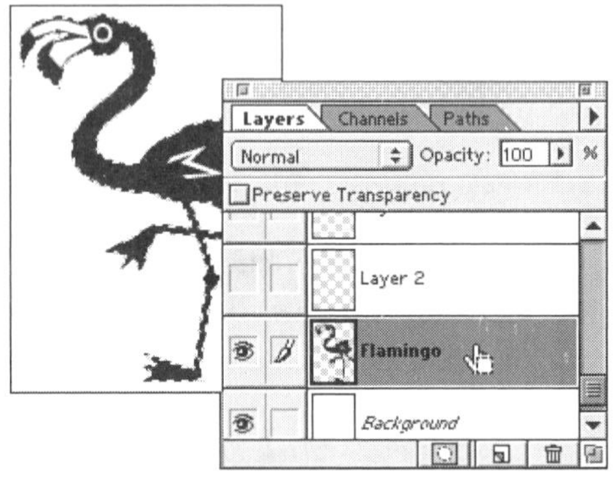

Add Layer Transparency to a Selection

Mac: Cmd-Shift-Click on layer

Win: Ctrl+Shift+Click on layer

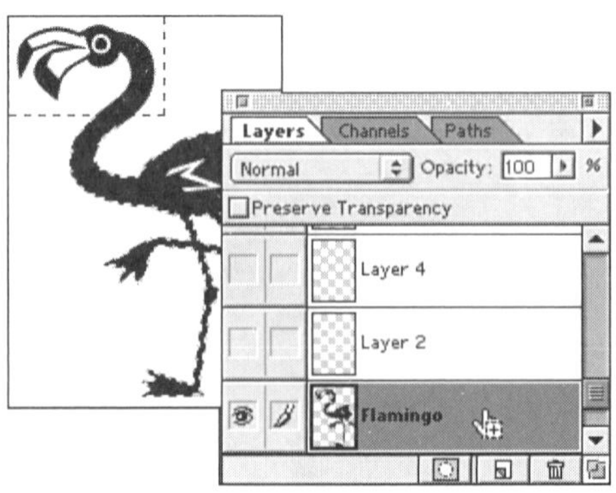

Subtract Layer Transparency from a Selection

Mac: Cmd-Option-Click on layer

Win: Ctrl+Alt+Click on layer

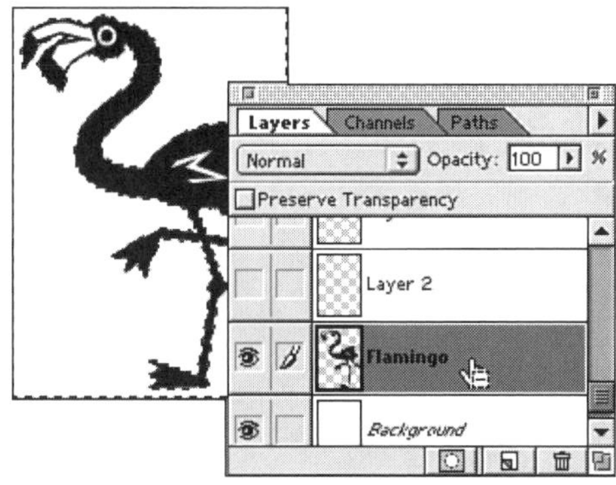

Intersect Layer Transparency with a Selection

Mac: Cmd-Option-Shift-Click on layer

Win: Ctrl+Alt+Shift+Click on layer

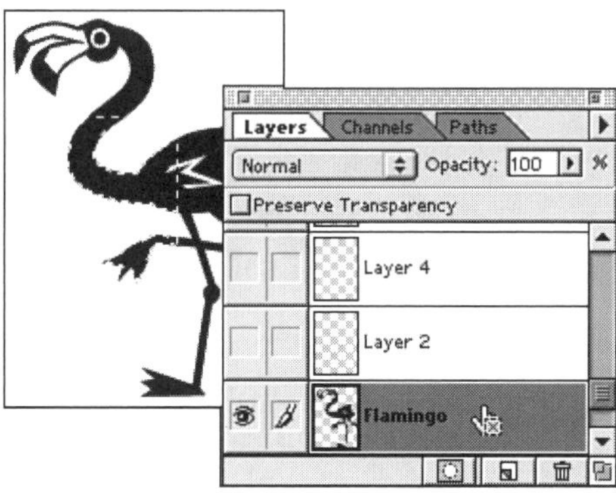

Layer Mask Commands

Create Layer Mask with Reveal All/Reveal Selection

Mouse: Click on Layer Mask button

Create Layer Mask with Hide All/Hide Selection

Mac: Option-Click on Layer Mask button

Win: Alt+Click on Layer Mask button

Toggle Layer Mask On/Off

Mouse: Shift+Click on layer mask thumbnail

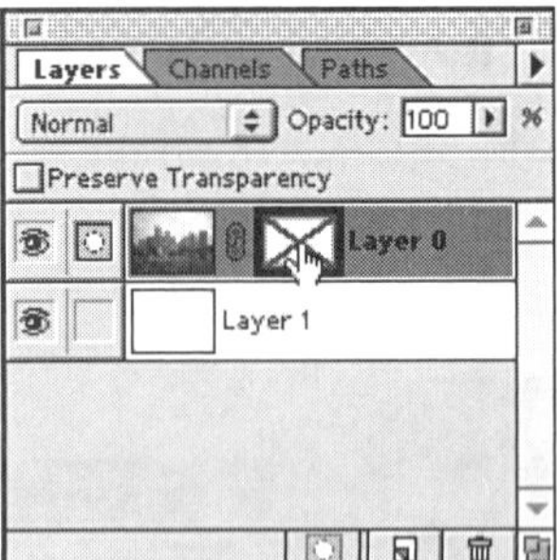

Toggle Between Layer Mask and Composite View

Mac: Option-Click on layer mask thumbnail

Win: Alt+Click on layer mask thumbnail

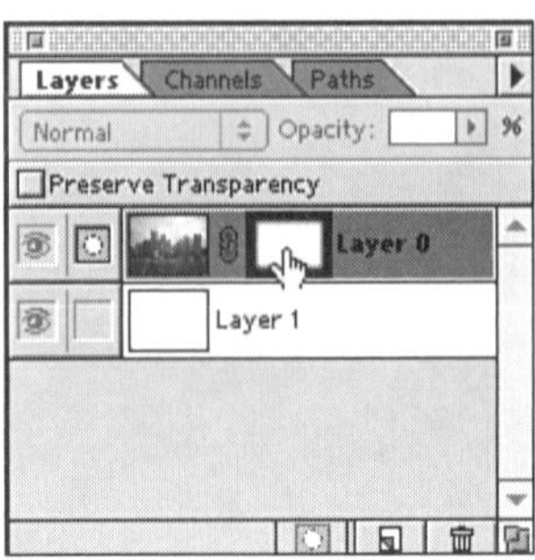

Toggle Rubylith (Mask Overlay) Mode for Layer Mask On/Off

Mac: Option-Shift-Click on layer mask thumbnail

Win: Alt+Shift+Click on layer mask thumbnail

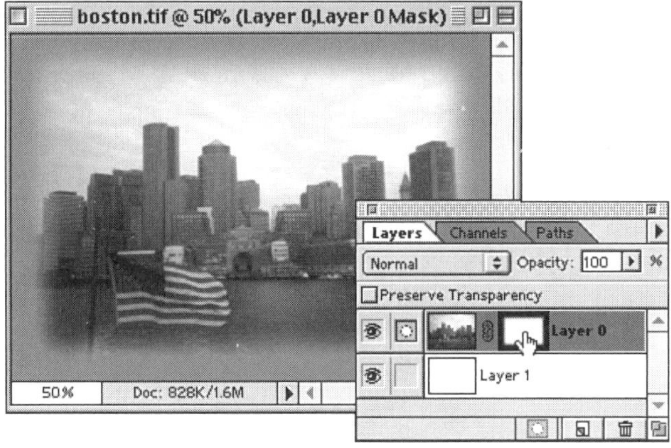

Link/Unlink a Layer Mask with Its Layer

Mouse: Click in the Link Layer Mask icon area

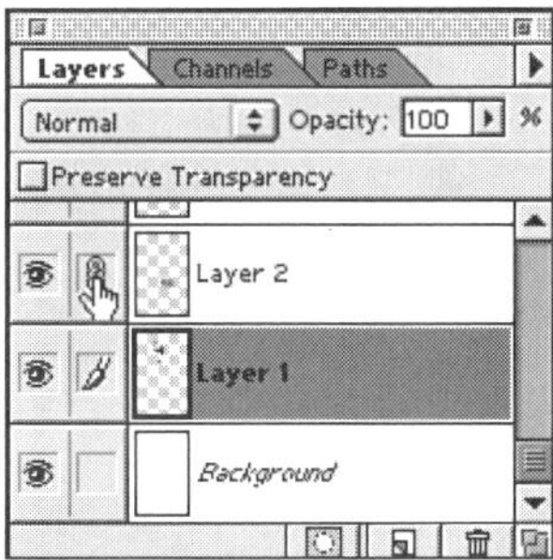

Open the Layer Mask Options Dialog Box

Mouse: Double-click on the Layer Mask icon

Layer Effects Commands

Clear Layer Effects

VERSION 5.0

Menu: Layer→Effects→Clear Effects

Mac: Option-Double-click effect icon

Win: Alt+Double-click effect icon

This shortcut removes one Layer Effect at a time, in the reverse order that you applied the effects to the layer.

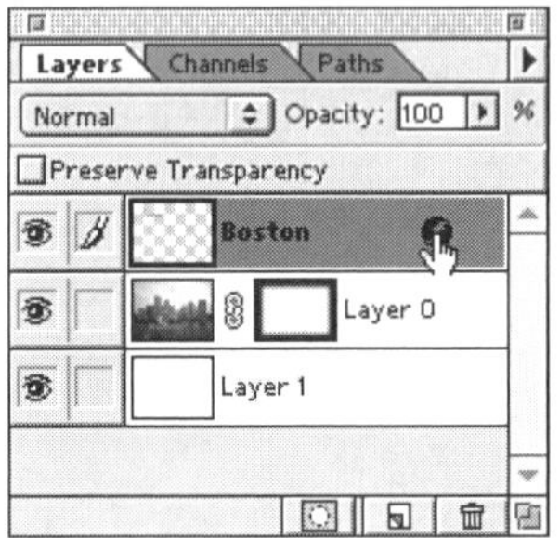

Edit Layer Effect Options

VERSION 5.0

Menu: Layer→Effects→Choose the effect to edit

Mouse: Double-click effect icon

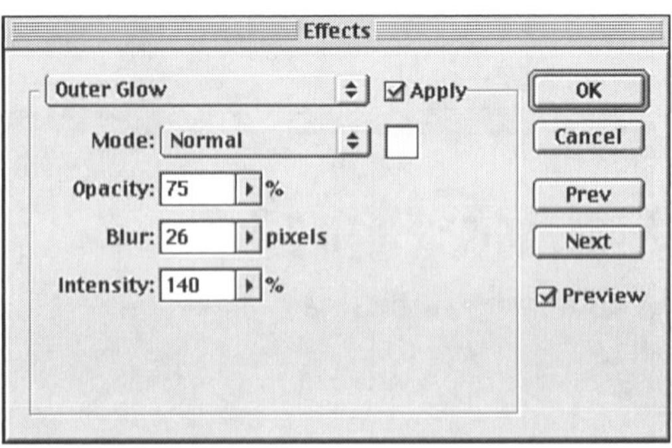

Toggle Effects On/Off Without Dialog Box

VERSION 5.0

Menu: Layer→Effects→desired effect

Mac: Option-Menu item

Win: Alt+Menu item

Reposition Effect While in Effect Dialog Box

VERSION 5.0

Mouse: Drag in the image window

Reposition Effect While in Effect Dialog Box Constrained to 45-Degree Axis

VERSION 5.0

Mouse: Shift+Drag in the image window

Switch to Drop Shadow Panel

VERSION 5.0

Mac: Cmd-1

Win: Ctrl+1

Switch to Inner Shadow Panel

VERSION 5.0

Mac: Cmd-2

Win: Ctrl+2

Switch to Outer Glow Panel

VERSION 5.0

Mac: Cmd-3

Win: Ctrl+3

Switch to Inner Glow Panel

VERSION 5.0

Mac: Cmd-4

Win: Ctrl+4

Switch to Bevel and Emboss Panel

VERSION 5.0

Mac: Cmd-5

Win: Ctrl+5

Switch to Color Fill Panel

VERSION 5.5

Mac: Cmd-6

Win: Ctrl+6

Type

Type Commands

Type Tool

Both: T

Cycle Through Type Tools

VERSION 5.0

Both: Shift+T

Apply and Exit from the Type Dialog Box

Both: Enter, NOT Return

Edit Type Options

VERSION 5.0

Both: Double-click Type icon or layer name

Reposition Type from Within Type Dialog Box

VERSION 5.0

Both: Press and drag in the image window

Toggle to Eyedropper Tool

Mac: Option

Win: Alt

This shortcut allows you to choose a new foreground color (and the color for the text you are about to create) before entering the Type dialog box and without having to switch tools first. This shortcut works with the Vertical Type tool as well.

Type Mask Commands

Add to Selection

Both: Shift+Click then drag

This shortcut works with the Vertical Type Mask tool as well.

Subtract from a Selection

Mac: Option-Click then drag

Win: Alt+Click then drag

This shortcut works with the Vertical Type Mask tool as well.

Intersect with a Selection

Mac: Option-Shift-Click then drag

Win: Alt+Shift+Click then drag

This shortcut works with the Vertical Type Mask tool as well.

Type Editing Commands

Cut, Copy, and Paste in the Type Dialog Box

VERSION 5.0

Mac: Cmd-X, Cmd-C, Cmd-V

Win: Ctrl+X, Ctrl+C, Ctrl+V

Move Cursor One Character Right

VERSION 5.0

Both: Right Arrow

Move Cursor One Character Left

VERSION 5.0

Both: Left Arrow

Move Cursor One Line Up

VERSION 5.0

Both: Up Arrow

Move Cursor One Line Down

VERSION 5.0

Both: Down Arrow

Move Cursor One Word Right

VERSION 5.0

Mac: Cmd-Right Arrow

Win: Ctrl+Right Arrow

Move Cursor One Word Left

VERSION 5.0

Mac: Cmd-Left Arrow

Win: Ctrl+Left Arrow

Editing a Type Layer

VERSION 5.0

Mouse: Click on the text with the Type tool

To edit a type layer, you usually double-click on the name of the layer in the Layers palette. However, you can also open the Type dialog box for a given type layer by using the Type tool. If you click on a transparent area with the Type tool, the Type dialog box opens, and whatever you type is placed on a new layer. If you click on the actual type in the layer, the Type dialog box opens with that specific text in it so that you can edit the existing type layer.

Constrain as You Reposition Type from Within the Type Dialog Box

VERSION 5.0

Mouse: Shift+Click and drag in the image window

Type Selection Commands

Select a Word

Mouse: Double-click on word

VERSION 5.0

Select One Character to the Right

Both: Shift+Right Arrow

VERSION 5.0

Select One Character to the Left

Both: Shift+Left Arrow

VERSION 5.0

Select One Word to the Right

Mac: Cmd-Shift-Right Arrow

Win: Ctrl+Shift+Right Arrow

VERSION 5.0

Select One Word to the Left

Mac: Cmd-Shift-Left Arrow

Win: Ctrl+Shift+Left Arrow

VERSION 5.0

Select One Line Up

Both: Shift+Up Arrow

VERSION 5.0

Select One Line Down

Both: Shift+Down Arrow

VERSION 5.0

Select All

VERSION 5.0

Mac: Cmd-A

Win: Ctrl+A

Select Characters from the Current Insertion Point

VERSION 5.0

Both: Shift+Click

Type Formatting Commands

Left/Top Text Alignment

VERSION 5.0

Mac: Cmd-Shift-L

Win: Ctrl+Shift+L

Center Text Alignment

VERSION 5.0

Mac: Cmd-Shift-C

Win: Ctrl+Shift+C

Right/Bottom Text Alignment

VERSION 5.0

Mac: Cmd-Shift-R

Win: Ctrl+Shift+R

Increase Text Point Size by 2 Points

VERSION 5.0

Mac: Cmd-Shift->

Win: Ctrl+Shift+>

Decrease Text Point Size by 2 Points

VERSION 5.0

Mac: Cmd-Shift-<

Win: Ctrl+Shift+<

Increase Text Point Size by 10 Points

VERSION 5.0

Mac: Cmd-Option-Shift->

Win: Ctrl+Alt+Shift+>

Decrease Text Point Size by 10 Points

VERSION 5.0

Mac: Cmd-Option-Shift-<

Win: Ctrl+Alt+Shift+<

Increase Leading by 2 Points

VERSION 5.0

Mac: Option-Down Arrow

Win: Alt+Down Arrow

Decrease Leading by 2 Points

VERSION 5.0

Mac: Option-Up Arrow

Win: Alt+Up Arrow

Increase Leading by 10 Points

VERSION 5.0

Mac: Cmd-Option-Down Arrow

Win: Ctrl+Alt+Down Arrow

Decrease Leading by 10 Points

VERSION 5.0

Mac: Cmd-Option-Up Arrow

Win: Ctrl+Alt+Up Arrow

Increase Kerning/Tracking by 2/100 Em Space

VERSION 5.0

Mac: Option-Right Arrow

Win: Alt+Right Arrow

Decrease Kerning/Tracking by 2/100 Em Space

VERSION 5.0

Mac: Option-Left Arrow

Win: Alt+Left Arrow

Increase Kerning/Tracking by 10/100 Em Space

VERSION 5.0

Mac: Cmd-Option-Right Arrow

Win: Ctrl+Alt+Right Arrow

Decrease Kerning/Tracking by 10/100 Em Space

VERSION 5.0

Mac: Cmd-Option-Left Arrow

Win: Ctrl+Alt+Left Arrow

Increase Baseline Shift by 2 Points

VERSION 5.0

Mac: Option-Shift-Up Arrow

Win: Alt+Shift+Up Arrow

Decrease Baseline Shift by 2 Points

VERSION 5.0

Mac: Option-Shift-Down Arrow

Win: Alt+Shift+Down Arrow

Increase Baseline Shift by 10 Points

VERSION 5.0

Mac: Cmd-Option-Shift-Up Arrow

Win: Ctrl+Alt+Shift+Up Arrow

Decrease Baseline Shift by 10 Points

VERSION 5.0

Mac: Cmd-Option-Shift-Down Arrow

Win: Ctrl+Alt+Shift+Down Arrow

Toggle Faux Bold Style

VERSION 5.5

Mac: Cmd-B

Win: Ctrl+B

Toggle Faux Italic Style

VERSION 5.5

Mac: Cmd-I

Win: Ctrl+I

Toggle Faux Underline Style

VERSION 5.5

Mac: Cmd-U

Win: Ctrl+U

Selections

Select Menu Commands

Move Selection Marquee 1 Pixel

Both: Arrow keys

Mouse: With a selection tool active, place cursor inside the selection, then press and drag

As long as a selection tool is active (Marquee, Lasso, Magic Wand), the arrow keys move just the selection marquee—not any pixels—one pixel in the direction of the arrow key you choose.

Move Selection Marquee 10 Pixels

Both: Shift+Arrow keys

Mouse: With a selection tool active, place cursor inside the selection, then press and drag

As long as a selection tool is active (Marquee, Lasso, Magic Wand), holding down the Shift key and then using the arrow keys moves a selection marquee 10 pixels in the direction of the arrow key you choose.

Move Selected Pixels 1 Pixel

Menu: Edit→Transform→Numeric

Both: Arrow keys

Mouse: With the Move tool active, press and drag

As long as the Move tool is active, the arrow keys move selected pixels one pixel in the direction of the arrow key you choose. If any other tool is active, hold down the (Cmd) [Ctrl] key, and then use the arrow keys.

Move Selected Pixels 10 Pixels

Menu: Edit→Transform→Numeric

Both: Shift+Arrow keys

Mouse: With the Move tool active, press and drag

As long as the Move tool is active, holding down the Shift key and then pressing the arrow keys moves selected pixels 10 pixels in the direction of the arrow key you choose. If any other tool is active, hold down the (Cmd-Shift) [Ctrl+Shift] keys, and then use the arrow keys.

Select All

Menu: Select→All

Mac: Cmd-A

Win: Ctrl+A

Deselect

Menu: Select→Deselect

Mac: Cmd-D

Win: Ctrl+D

Reselect

Menu: Select→Reselect

Mac: Cmd-Shift-D

Win: Ctrl+Shift+D

Inverse

Menu: Select→Inverse

Mac: Cmd-Shift-I

Win: Ctrl+Shift+I

Feather

Menu: Select→Feather

Mac: Cmd-Option-D

Win: Ctrl+Option+D

Transform a Selection

VERSION 4.0

Menu: Select→Transform Selection

Mac: Cmd-Option-T

Win: Ctrl+Alt+T

This shortcut only works in Photoshop 4. To use the Transform Selection command in Photoshop 5/5.5, you must use the menu command, or assign the menu command to an F key using Actions.

Load Layer Transparency as a Selection

Mac: Cmd-Click on layer

Win: Ctrl+Click on layer

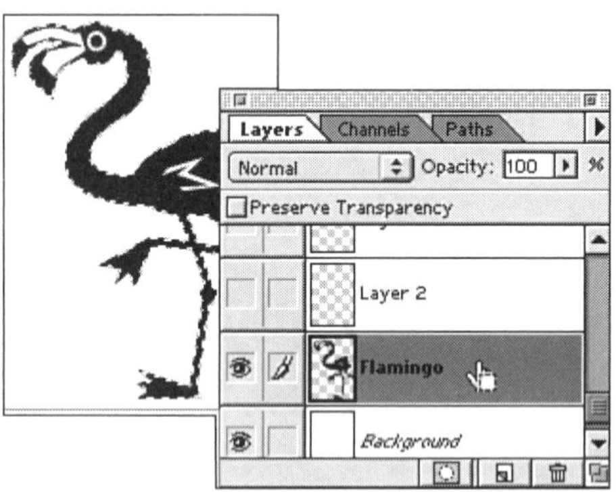

Add Layer Transparency to a Selection

Mac: Cmd-Shift-Click on layer

Win: Ctrl+Shift+Click on layer

Subtract Layer Transparency from a Selection

Mac: Cmd-Option-Click on layer

Win: Ctrl+Alt+Click on layer

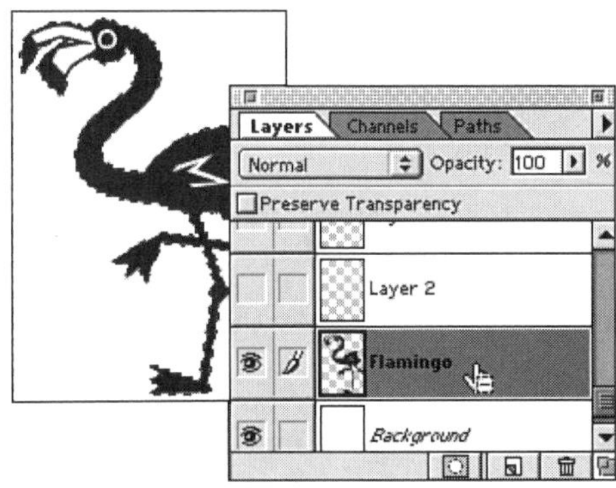

Intersect Layer Transparency with a Selection

Mac: Cmd-Option-Shift-Click on layer

Win: Ctrl+Alt+Shift+Click on layer

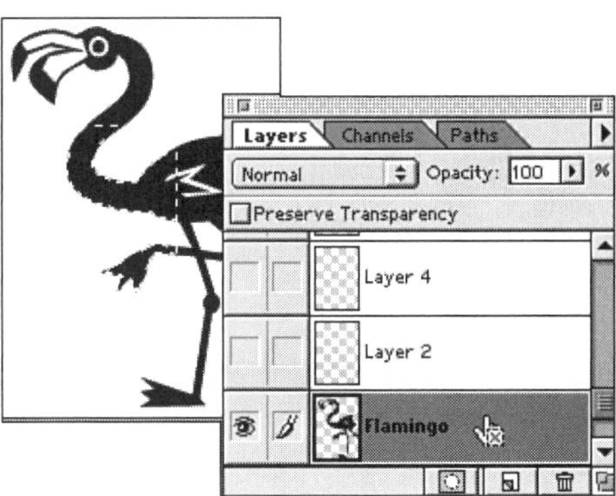

Selection Tool Shortcuts

Add to a Selection

Mouse: Shift+Drag

This shortcut is the same when using any of the selection tools: Rectangular Marquee, Elliptical Marquee, or any of the Lasso tools.

Subtract from a Selection

Mac: Option-Drag

Win: Alt+Drag

This shortcut is the same when using any of the selection tools: Rectangular Marquee, Elliptical Marquee, or any of the Lasso tools.

Intersect with a Selection

Mac: Option-Shift-Drag

Win: Alt+Shift+Drag

This shortcut is the same when using any of the selection tools: Rectangular Marquee, Elliptical Marquee, or any of the Lasso tools.

Constrain to a Square Selection

Mouse: Shift+Drag

This shortcut only works if you are starting a new selection. If a selection already exists, you add to the selection instead.

Constrain to a Circle Selection

Mouse: Shift+Drag

This shortcut only works if you are starting a new selection. If a selection already exists, you add to the selection instead.

Draw from the Center While Creating Selections

Mac: Option-Drag

Win: Alt+Drag

Normally, when creating a selection, the selection anchors itself from wherever you click, creating the selection outward from that position in a diagonal direction. With this shortcut, wherever you click becomes the center of the selection as you create it. Also, remember that this shortcut only works if you are starting a new selection. If a selection already exists, you subtract from the selection instead.

Constrain and Draw from the Center While Creating Selections

Mac: Option-Shift-Drag

Win: Alt+Shift+Drag

Normally, when creating a selection, the selection anchors itself from wherever you click, creating the selection outward from that position in a diagonal direction. With this shortcut, wherever you click becomes the center of the selection as you create it. Also, remember that this shortcut only works if you are starting a new selection. If a selection already exists, you are left with the intersection of the selections instead.

Constrain a Selection as You Move It

Mouse: Shift+Drag

Make sure the cursor is within the selection area and that you press the mouse button down before you hold down the Shift key. If you hold down the Shift key first, you will add to the selection when you start dragging. If the cursor is outside the selected area, you will start a new selection instead of moving the existing one.

Reposition a Selection as You Create It

Both: Spacebar

This is one of my favorite shortcuts. Sometimes you are trying to select a specific shape in an image and halfway through dragging out the selection, you realize you didn't start in the right position. Rather than starting over, just hold down the Spacebar. This allows you to drag the marquee to a different position. When you are ready to continue with the selection, just let go of the Spacebar. Remember to keep the mouse button down until you are finished making the selection.

Duplicate a Selection

Mac: Option-Drag

Win: Alt+Drag

Draw Using the Polygonal Lasso Tool

Mac: Option-Click/Drag

Win: Alt+Click/Drag

This shortcut allows you to temporarily switch to the Polygonal Lasso tool while using the regular Lasso tool.

Draw Using the Lasso Tool

Mac: Option-Click/Drag

Win: Alt+Click/Drag

This shortcut allows you to temporarily switch to the Lasso tool while using the Polygonal Lasso tool.

Magnetic Lasso Shortcuts

Add to a Selection

Mouse: Shift+Click then draw — VERSION 5.0

This shortcut is the same when using any of the selection tools: Rectangular Marquee, Elliptical Marquee, or any of the Lasso tools.

Subtract from a Selection

Mac: Option-Click then draw — VERSION 5.0

Win: Alt+Click then draw

This shortcut is the same when using any of the selection tools: Rectangular Marquee, Elliptical Marquee, or any of the Lasso tools.

Intersect with a Selection

Mac: Option-Shift-Click then draw — VERSION 5.0

Win: Alt+Shift+Click then draw

This shortcut is the same when using any of the selection tools: Rectangular Marquee, Elliptical Marquee, or any of the Lasso tools.

Add a Point

Mouse: Single-click — VERSION 5.0

Delete the Last Point

Both: Delete — VERSION 5.0

Close the Selection

Both: Double-click or Enter — VERSION 5.0

Close the Selection at the Starting Point

VERSION 5.0

Mouse: Click on the starting point

Close the Selection Using a Straight-Line Segment

VERSION 5.0

Mac: Option-Double-click

Win: Alt+Double-click

Cancel the Operation

VERSION 5.0

Mac: Cmd-. (period)

Win: Ctrl+. (period)

Both: Escape

Switch to Lasso Tool

VERSION 5.0

Mac: Option-Drag

Win: Alt+Drag

Increase Magnetic Lasso Width

VERSION 5.0

Both:]

Decrease Magnetic Lasso Width

VERSION 5.0

Both: [

Magic Wand Shortcuts

Add to a Selection

Mouse: Shift+Click

Subtract from a Selection

Mac: Option-Click

Win: Alt+Click

Intersect with a Selection

Mac: Option-Shift-Click

Win: Alt+Shift+Click

Channels

Show or Hide a Channel

Mouse: Click in Eye icon area

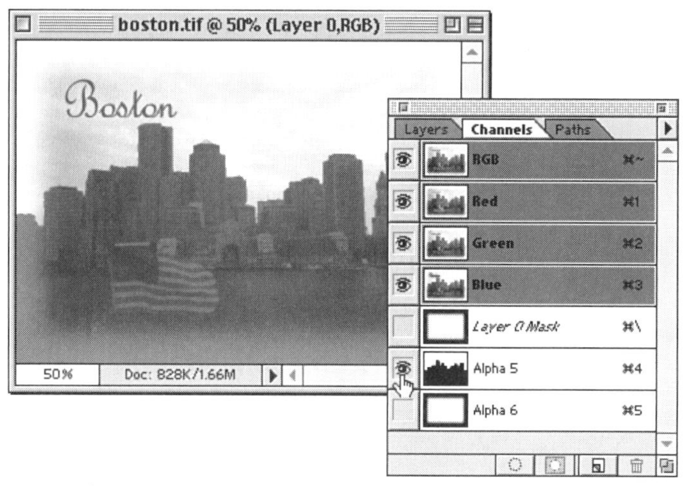

Target Individual Channels

Mac: Cmd-[1–9]

Win: Ctrl+[1–9]

Both: Click on desired channel thumbnail

With these shortcuts, you target an individual channel without having to use the Channels palette. Hold down the specified modifier key and then press the number of the channel you want to target. For instance, in an RGB file, the first three channels in the file are the red, green, and blue channels, respectively. (Cmd-1) [Ctrl+1] targets the red channel, (Cmd-2) [Ctrl+2] targets the green channel, and so on. (Cmd-4) [Ctrl+4] targets the first of any alpha channels you have created in the file. You can target the first nine channels in the file using the 1–9 keys.

Note: If you click on the composite channel, this in effect turns on the individual channels that make up the composite channel.

Target the Composite Channel

Mac: Cmd-~ (tilde)

Win: Ctrl+~ (tilde)

To return to the composite channel, hold down the appropriate modifier key and press the tilde key—it's the key to the left of the number 1 key.

Create a New Channel

Mouse: Click on the New Channel button

Clicking the New Channel button in the Channels palette skips the New Channel dialog box when creating a new channel. Channels are automatically named (Alpha 1, Alpha 2, and so on).

Create a New Channel with the New Channel Dialog Box

Mac: Option-Click the New Channel button in the Channels palette

Win: Alt+Click the New Channel button in the Channels palette

This shortcut opens the New Channel dialog box and gives you a chance to name the new channel and specify other options as well.

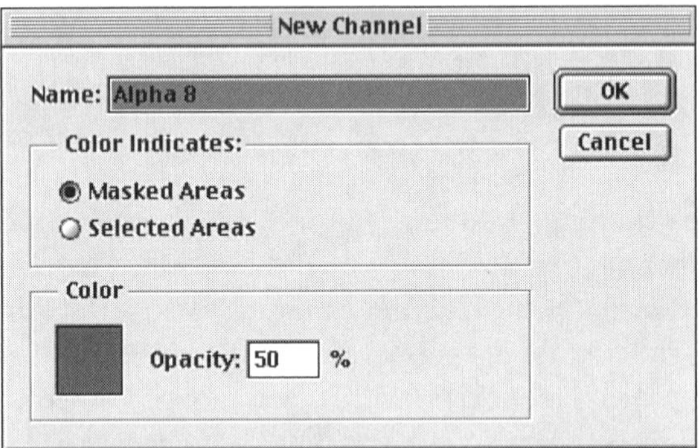

Duplicate a Channel

Mouse: Drag the channel to the New Channel button

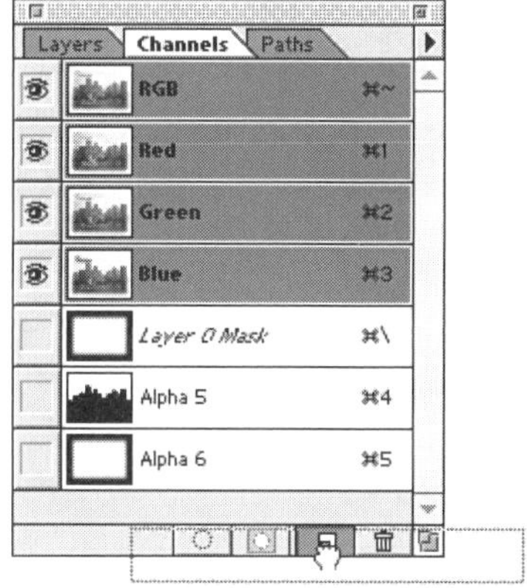

Delete a Channel

Mouse: Click the Delete Channel button

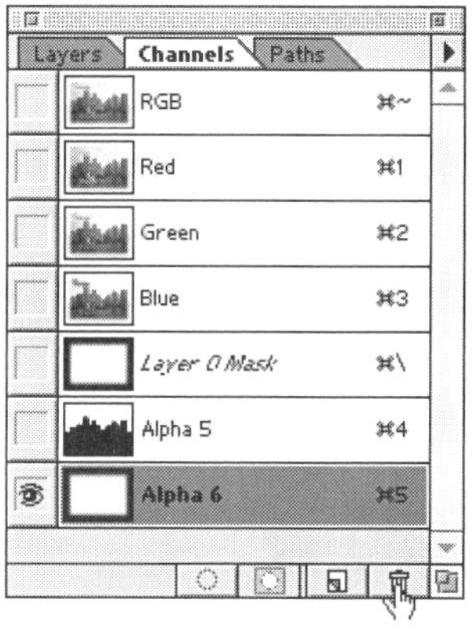

Delete a Channel and Skip the Warning Alert

Mac: Option-Click the Delete Channel button

Win: Alt+Click the Delete Channel button

Create a New Spot Color Channel

VERSION 5.0

Mac: Cmd-Click the New Channel button

Win: Ctrl+Click the New Channel button

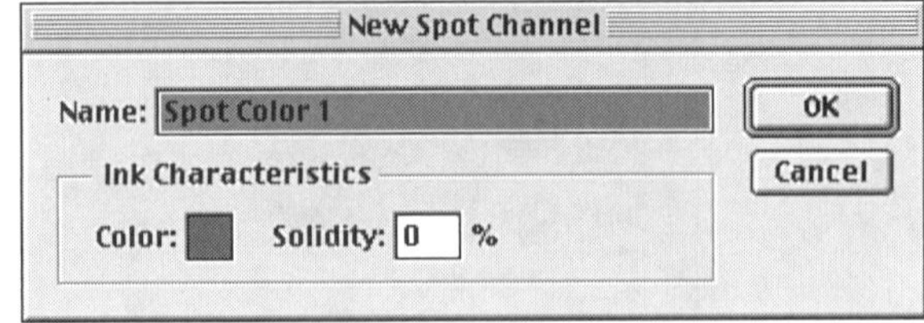

Save a Selection as a Channel

Menu: Select→Save Selection

Mouse: Click the Save Selection button

Clicking the Save Selection button in the Channels palette skips the New Channel dialog box when creating a new channel. Channels are automatically named (Alpha 1, Alpha 2, and so on).

Load a Channel as a Selection

Menu: Select→Load Selection

Mac: Cmd-Option-[1–9] or Cmd-Click on the desired channel

Win: Ctrl+Alt+[1–9] or Ctrl+Click on the desired channel

Mouse: Target desired channel and then click Load Channel as Selection button

With these shortcuts, you can load an individual channel as a selection without having to use the Channels palette. Hold down the specified modifier keys and then press the number of the channel you want to load. For instance, in an RGB file, the first three channels in the file are the red, green, and blue channels, respectively. (Cmd-Option-1) [Ctrl+Alt+1] loads the red channel, (Cmd-Option-2) [Ctrl+Alt+2] loads the green channel, and so on. (Cmd-Option-4) [Ctrl +Alt+4] loads the first of any alpha channels you have created in the file. You can load the first nine channels in the file using the 1–9 keys.

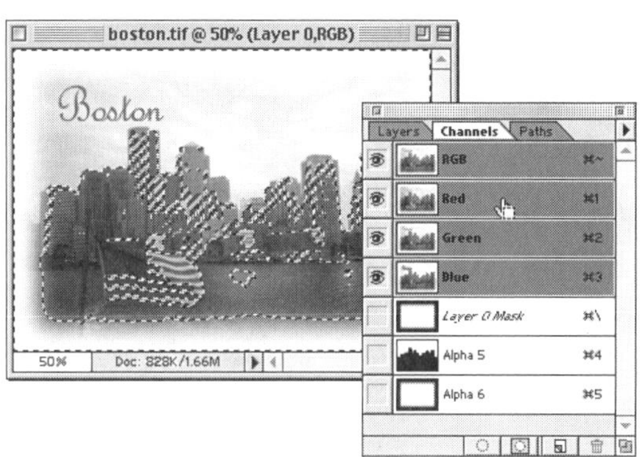

Save a Selection as a Channel with the New Channel Dialog Box

Menu: Select→Save Selection

Mac: Option-Click the Save Selection button

Win: Alt+Click the Save Selection button

This shortcut opens the New Channel dialog box and gives you a chance to name the new channel and specify other options as well.

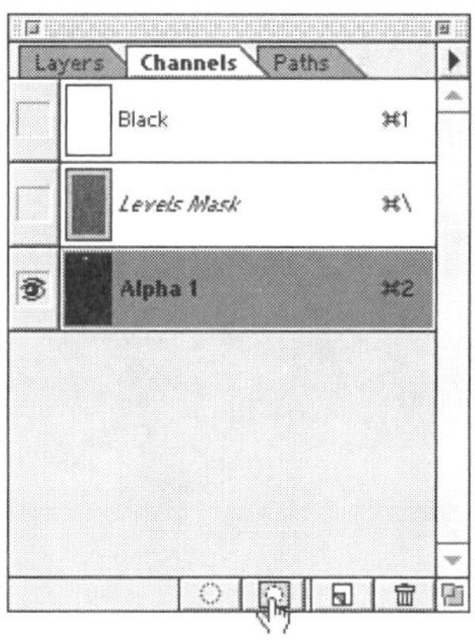

Add a Channel to a Selection

Menu: Select→Load Selection

Mac: Cmd-Shift-Click on the channel thumbnail

Win: Ctrl+Shift+Click on the channel thumbnail

Both: Shift+Click on the Load Selection button

Subtract a Channel from a Selection

Menu: Select→Load Selection

Mac: Cmd-Option-Click on the channel thumbnail

Win: Ctrl+Alt+Click on the channel thumbnail

Both: (Option-Click) on the Load Selection button; [Alt+Click] on the Load Selection button

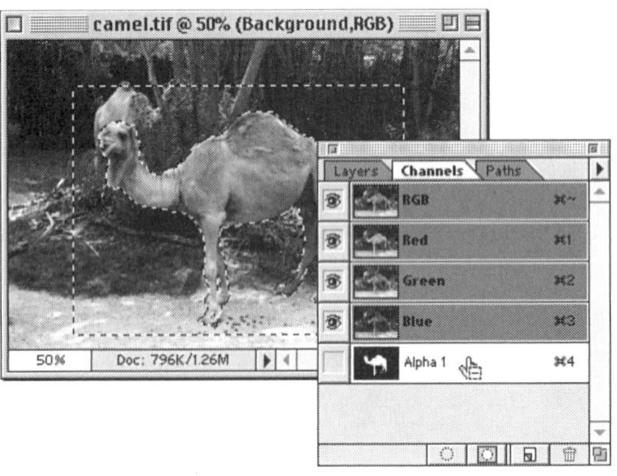

Intersect a Channel with a Selection

Menu: Select→Load Selection

Mac: Cmd-Option-Shift-Click on the channel thumbnail

Win: Ctrl+Alt+Shift+Click on the channel thumbnail

Both: (Option-Shift-Click) on the Load Selection button; [Alt+Shift+Click] on the Load Selection button

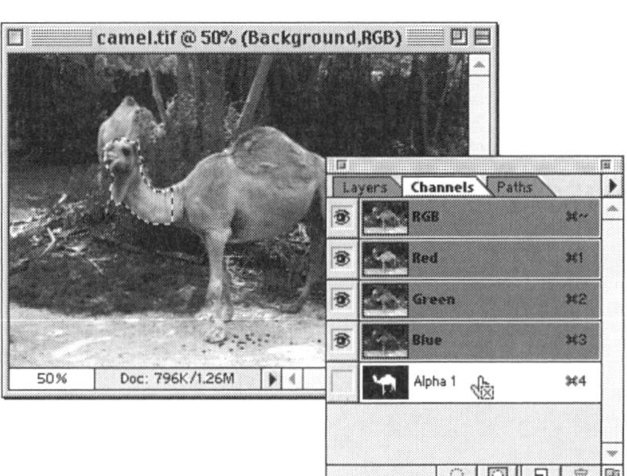

View a Color Channel Without Hiding Other Color Channels

Mouse: Shift+Click on the channel name

Edit Channel Options

Mouse: Double-click on desired channel

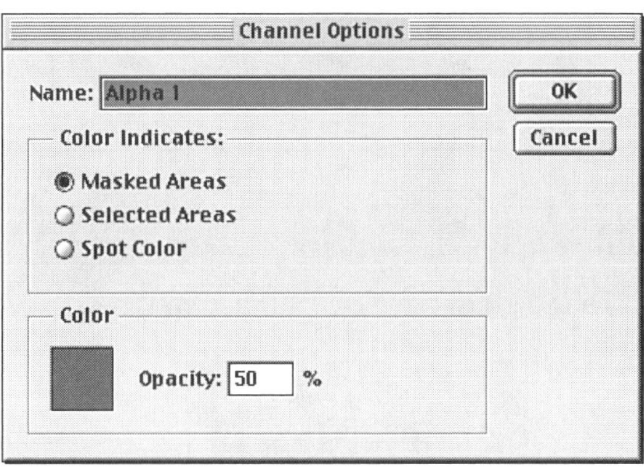

Paths

Create a New Path

Mouse: Click the New Path button

Clicking the New Path button in the Paths palette skips the New Path dialog box when creating a new path. Paths are automatically named (Path 1, Path 2, and so on).

Create a New Path with the New Path Dialog Box

Mac: Option-Click the New Path button in the Paths palette

Win: Alt+Click the New Path button in the Paths palette

This shortcut opens the New Path dialog box and gives you a chance to name the new path as you create it.

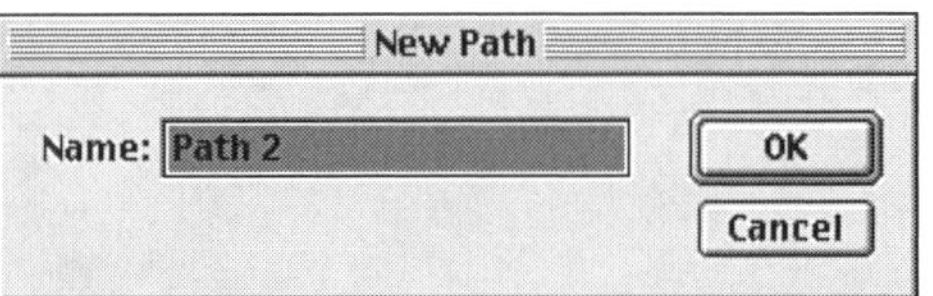

Duplicate a Path

Mouse: Drag path to the New Path button

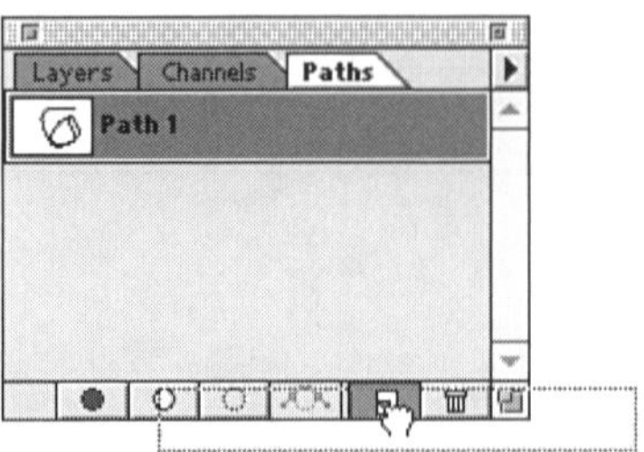

Duplicate a Path

Mac: Option-Drag path

Win: Alt+Drag path

Delete a Path

Mouse: Click the Delete Path button

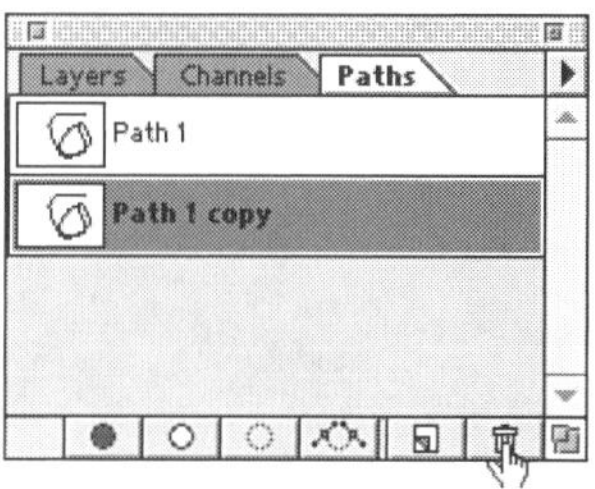

Delete a Path and Skip the Warning Alert

Mac: Option-Click the Delete Path button

Win: Alt+Click the Delete Path button

Draw Path Constrained to 45-Degree Axis

Mouse: Shift+Click/Drag

Add or Delete Anchor Points

Mouse: Click on path or anchor points

VERSION 5.0

Select Multiple Anchor Points

Mouse: Shift+Click

Edit a Pathname

Mouse: Double-click pathname

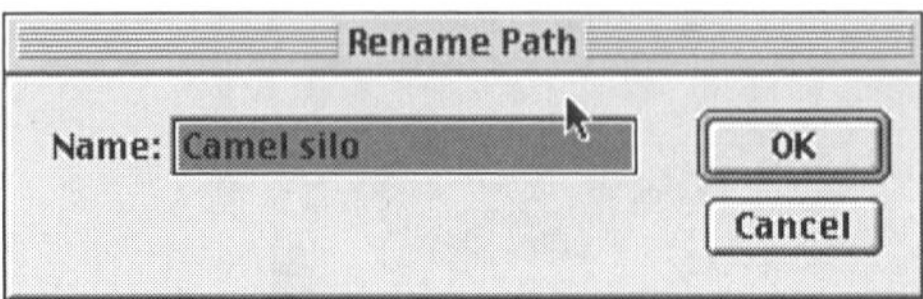

Add a Path to a Selection

Mac: Cmd-Shift-Click on the path thumbnail

Win: Ctrl+Shift+Click on the path thumbnail

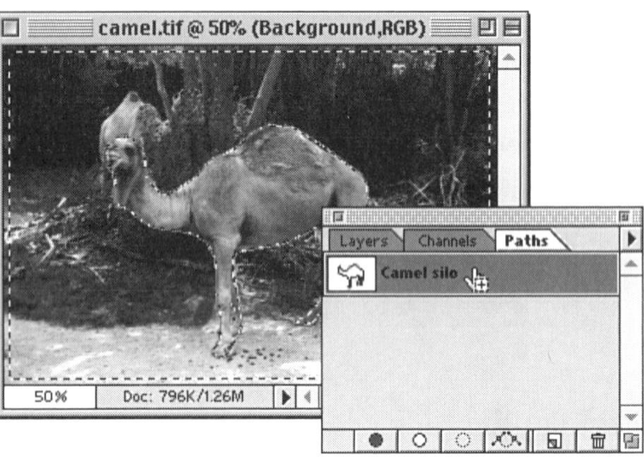

Subtract a Path from a Selection

Mac: Cmd-Option-Click on the path thumbnail

Win: Ctrl+Alt+Click on the path thumbnail

Intersect a Path with a Selection

Mac: Cmd-Option-Shift-Click on the path thumbnail

Win: Ctrl+Alt+Shift+Click on the path thumbnail

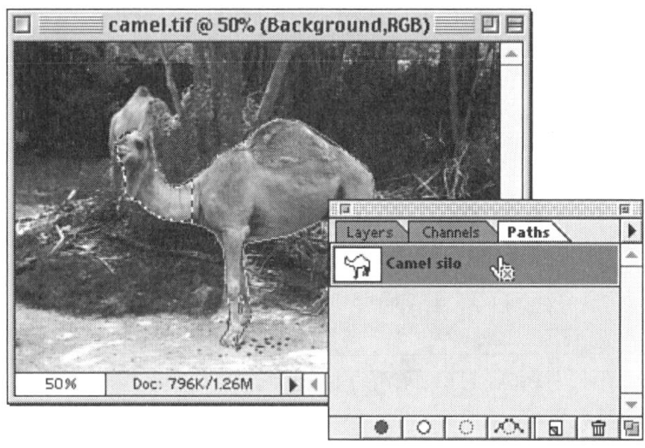

Stroke a Path with the Foreground Color

Mouse: Click the Stroke Path button

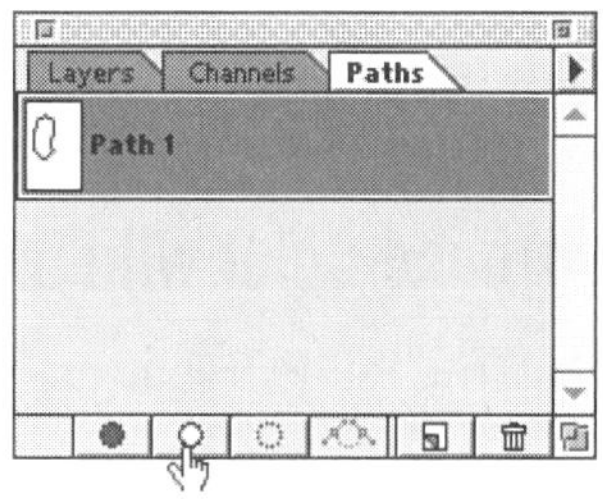

Stroke a Path with the Foreground Color with the Stroke Path Dialog Box

Mac: Option-Click the Stroke Path button

Win: Alt+Click the Stroke Path button

This shortcut opens the Stroke Path dialog box and allows you to specify which tool setting you want used to apply the stroke to the path.

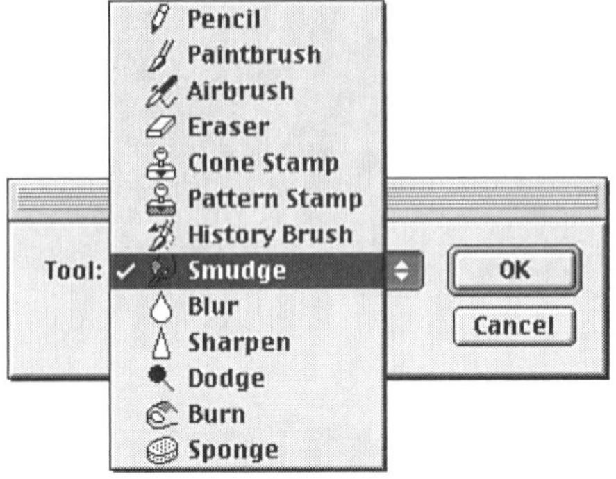

Fill a Path with the Foreground Color

Mouse: Click the Fill Path button

Fill a Path with the Foreground Color with the Fill Path Dialog Box

Mac: Option-Click the Fill Path button

Win: Alt+Click the Fill Path button

This shortcut opens the Fill Path dialog box and allows you to specify fill options such as opacity, blend mode, feathering, and so on.

Convert Work Path into a Saved Path

Mouse: Double-click on the pathname or drag Work Path to the New Path button

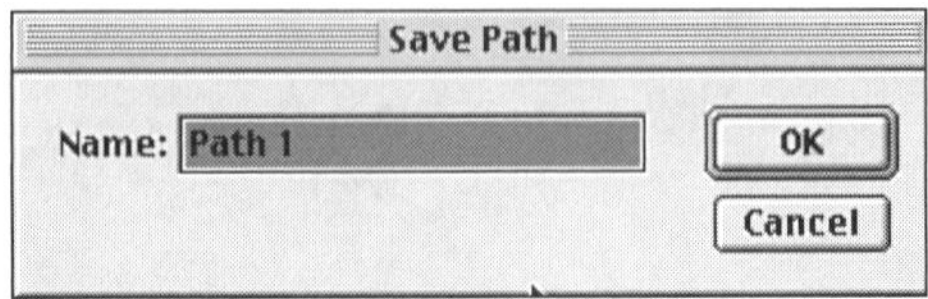

Load Path as a Selection

Mac: Cmd-Click on the path thumbnail

Win: Ctrl+Click on the path thumbnail

Both: Enter or click the Load Selection button

Convert Path into a Selection with the Make Selection Dialog Box

Mac: Option-Click the Load Selection button

Win: Alt+Click the Load Selection button

This shortcut opens the Make Selection dialog box and allows you to specify options for the selection, such as a feathering radius.

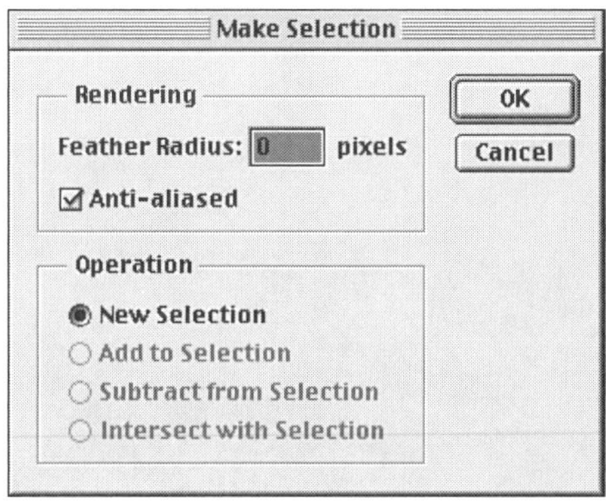

Convert Selection into a Path

Mouse: Click the Make Work Path button

Convert Selection into a Path with the Work Path Dialog Box

Mac: Option-Click the Make Work Path button

Win: Alt+Click the Make Work Path button

This shortcut opens the Make Work Path dialog box and allows you to specify options for the path.

Magnetic Pen Tool Shortcuts

Add a Point

VERSION 5.0

Mouse: Single-click

Delete the Last Point

VERSION 5.0

Both: Delete

Close the Path

VERSION 5.0

Both: Double-click or Enter

Close the Path at the Starting Point

VERSION 5.0

Mouse: Click on the starting point

Close the Path Using a Straight-Line Segment

VERSION 5.0

Mac: Option-Double-click

Win: Alt+Double-click

Cancel the Operation

VERSION 5.0

Mac: Cmd-. (period)

Win: Ctrl+. (period)

Both: Escape

Draw with (Switch to) the Freeform Pen Tool

VERSION 5.0

Mac: Option-Drag

Win: Alt+Drag

Draw with (Switch to) the Pen Tool

VERSION 5.0

Mac: Option-Click

Win: Alt+Click

Increase Magnetic Pen Width

VERSION 5.0

Both:]

Decrease Magnetic Pen Width

VERSION 5.0

Both: [

Type Selection Shortcuts

Select a Word

Mouse: Double-click on word

VERSION 5.0

Select One Character to the Right

Both: Shift+Right Arrow

VERSION 5.0

Select One Character to the Left

Both: Shift+Left Arrow

VERSION 5.0

Select One Word to the Right

Mac: Cmd-Shift-Right Arrow

Win: Ctrl+Shift+Right Arrow

VERSION 5.0

Select One Word to the Left

Mac: Cmd-Shift-Left Arrow

Win: Ctrl+Shift+Left Arrow

VERSION 5.0

Select One Line Up

Both: Shift+Up Arrow

VERSION 5.0

Select One Line Down

Both: Shift+Down Arrow

VERSION 5.0

Select All

VERSION 5.0

Mac: Cmd-A

Win: Ctrl+A

Select Characters from Current Insertion Point

VERSION 5.0

Both: Shift+Click

The **Filters** Menu

Filter Commands

Repeat the Last Filter Used

Menu: Filter→Name of the filter

Mac: Cmd-F

Win: Ctrl+F

This shortcut just applies the last filter you used again; it does not reopen the dialog box of the filter you used last so that you can change the settings before applying again. As you might guess, there is a separate shortcut for that as well.

Reopen the Last Filter Used with Same Settings

Mac: Cmd-Option-F

Win: Ctrl+Alt+F

Fade the Last Filter Used

Menu: Filter→Fade name of the filter

Mac: Cmd-Shift-F

Win: Ctrl+Shift+F

This is a great shortcut to knock back the intensity of a particular effect if you think it modified the image too strongly by playing with the opacity and/or the blend mode of the applied filter effect.

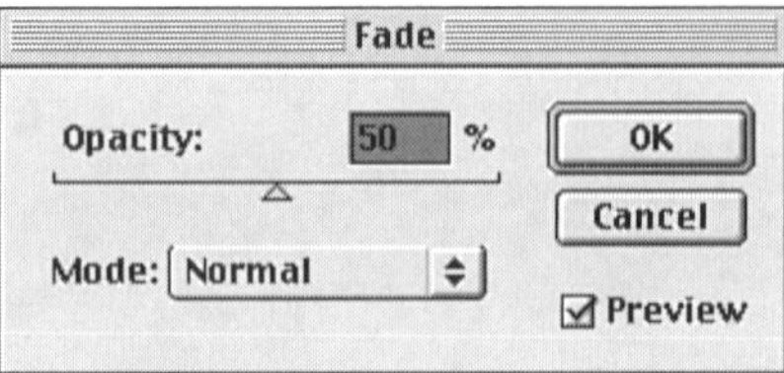

3D Transform Filter

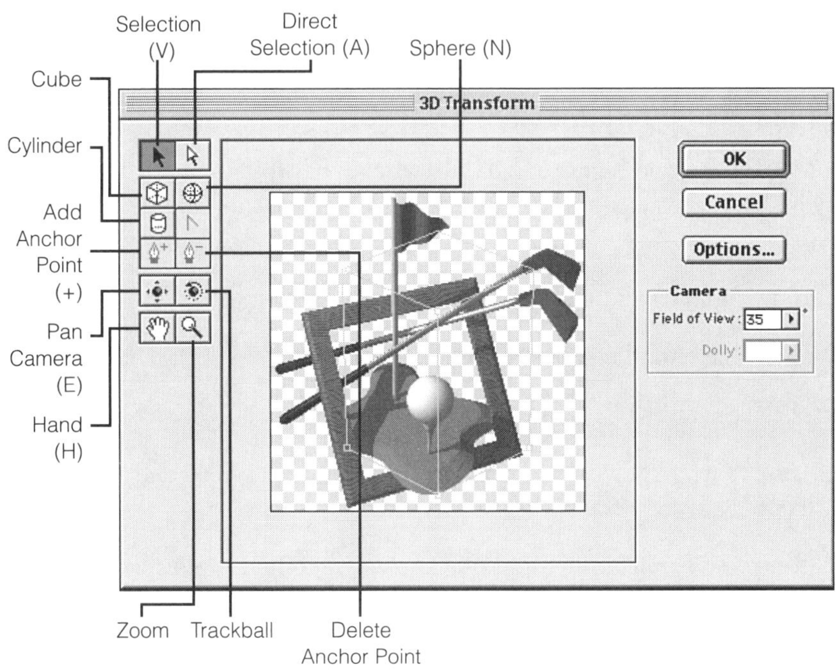

Toggle Between Select/Direct Select Tools

VERSION 5.0

Mac: Cmd-Tab

Win: Ctrl+Tab

If you are using Mac OS 8.5 or higher, see the tip "Changing the Mac OS Application Switcher," later in this chapter, to override the system's use of the Cmd-Tab shortcut.

Pan Image

VERSION 5.0

Mouse: Spacebar+Drag

Zoom In

VERSION 5.0

Mac: Cmd-Spacebar-Click/Drag

Win: Ctrl+Spacebar+Click/Drag

Zoom Out

VERSION 5.0

Mac: Option-Spacebar-Click/Drag

Win: Alt+Spacebar+Click/Drag

Changing the Mac OS Application Switcher

In Mac OS 8.5 and higher, Cmd-Tab switches between open applications. To disable this so you can use Photoshop's Cmd-Tab shortcuts, follow these steps:

1. In the Finder, choose Help→Mac OS Help.
2. Click "Files and Programs" in the left pane.
3. Click "Switching between open programs" in the right pane.
4. Scroll down to "Switching from one program to another" and click "Help me modify the keyboard shortcuts."
5. A dialog box might appear asking you where to find the Application Switcher. If so, navigate to the Extensions folder inside your System folder and double-click the Application Switcher.
6. Another dialog box will appear asking you if you want to use the keyboard shortcut to switch between applictions. Click No.

Lighting Effects

Duplicate Light in Lighting Effects Preview

Mac: Option-Drag light

Win: Alt+Drag light

Delete Light in Lighting Effects Preview

Both: Delete

Adjust Light Footprint Without Changing the Angle

Mouse: Shift+Drag handle

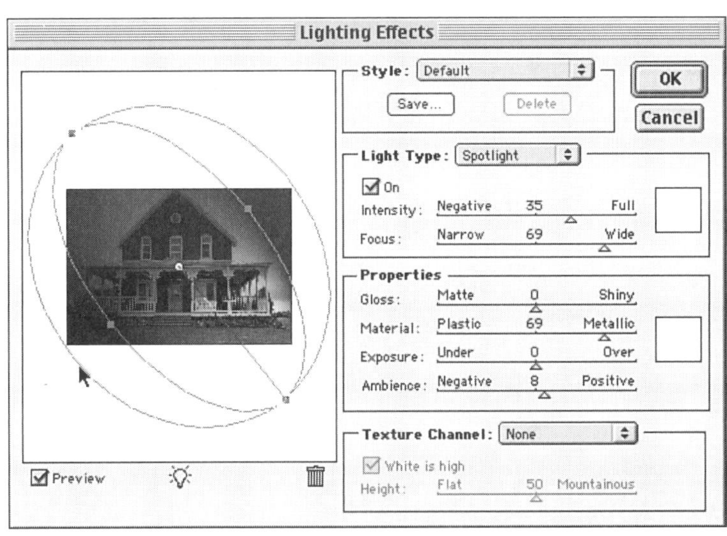

Adjust Light Angle Without Changing the Footprint

Mac: Cmd-Drag handle

Win: Ctrl+Drag handle

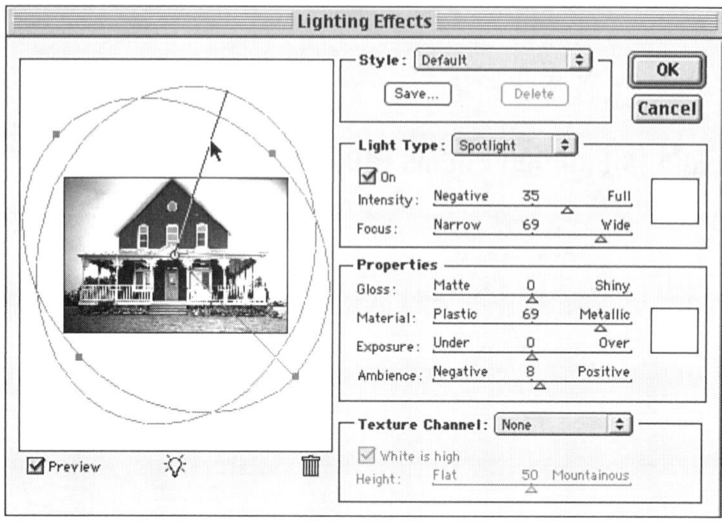

The **View** Menu

View Menu Commands

Preview Gamut Warning

Menu: View→Gamut Warning

Mac: Cmd-Shift-Y

Win: Ctrl+Shift+Y

Preview CMYK

Menu: View→Preview→CMYK

Mac: Cmd-Y

Win: Ctrl+Y

Hide Edges

Menu: View→Hide Edges

Mac: Cmd-H

Win: Ctrl+H

Hide Path

Menu: View→Hide Path

Mac: Cmd-Shift-H

Win: Ctrl+Shift+H

Toggle Show/Hide Rulers

Menu: View→Show/Hide Rulers

Mac: Cmd-R

Win: Ctrl+R

Toggle Show/Hide Guides

Menu: View→Show/Hide Guides

Mac: Cmd-; (semicolon)

Win: Ctrl+; (semicolon)

Toggle Snap to Guides

Menu: View→Snap to Guides

Mac: Cmd-Shift-; (semicolon)

Win: Ctrl+Shift+; (semicolon)

Toggle Lock/Unlock Guides

Menu: View→Lock Guides

Mac: Cmd-Option-; (semicolon)

Win: Ctrl+Alt+; (semicolon)

Toggle Show/Hide Grid

Menu: View→Show Grid

Mac: Cmd-' (apostrophe)

Win: Ctrl+' (apostrophe)

Toggle Snap to Grid

Menu: View→Snap to Grid

Mac: Cmd-Shift-' (apostrophe)

Win: Ctrl+Shift+' (apostrophe)

Snap Guide to Ruler

Mouse: Shift-Drag guide

Toggle Guide Orientation

Mac: Option-Drag guide

Win: Alt+Drag guide

The **Window** Menu

Window Menu Commands

Show or Hide the Info Palette

Menu: Window→Show/Hide Info

Both: F8

Show the Options Palette

Menu: Window→Show/Hide Options

Both: Enter or Return

Mouse: Double-click on a tool

Show or Hide the Color Palette

Menu: Window→Show/Hide Color

Both: F6

Show or Hide the Swatches Palette

Menu: Window→Show/Hide Swatches

Both: F6

F6 shows or hides the Color palette. Also use it to show or hide the Swatches palette. To show Swatches if the Color palette is not open, press F6, and then click on the Swatches tab. To hide both the Swatches and the Color palettes, press the F6 key until they both disappear.

Show or Hide the Brushes Palette

Menu: Window→Show/Hide Brushes

Both: F5

Show or Hide the Layers Palette

Menu: Window→Show/Hide Layers

Both: F7

Show or Hide the Channels Palette

Menu: Window→Show/Hide Channels

Both: F7

F7 shows or hides the Layers palette. Also use it to show or hide the Channels palette. To show Channels if the Layers palette is not open, press F7, and then click on the Channels tab. To hide both the Channels and the Layers palettes, press the F7 key until they both disappear.

Steal the Attributes of an Open Document

Menu: Window→Choose the document from the list

Here is another one of those deeply buried, not obvious, and undocumented shortcuts that make you say, "Doh! I wish I knew that years ago!" When you are compositing images together, it is often useful to make the canvas sizes of all the documents you are using the same. There are three different places you can take advantage of this trick: the New dialog box, the Image Size dialog box, and the Canvas Size dialog box. When in any of these three places, you may have never noticed that most of the menus are grayed out and unavailable. However, the Window menu is available. If you choose any open document listed in the Window menu, Photoshop automatically changes the attributes of the New, Image Size, and Canvas Size dialog boxes to match the open document.

PART TWO

ImageReady

Palettes

Palettes

Working Efficiently with Palettes

You know you are living large when you are working in ImageReady with dual monitors—one for the document window, and one for all the palettes. For those of us who don't have two monitors, my general strategy for arranging the palettes is to group them in such a way that I can access any and all of the palettes using the default Function key assignments. In other words, not every palette has a Function key assigned to it, but as long as a given palette is grouped with a palette that does have a Function key assigned to it, you can get to that palette without having pull down the menu.

When I watch people working in ImageReady, two of the most inefficient habits that I see include constantly moving palettes all over the screen and overlapping the palettes so that sometimes a palette gets hidden behind another palette. I overcome this by arranging the palettes on the screen the way you see them in the figure, and then leaving them there. I never (hardly) move them from these positions. I just leave them open all the time. If they are in the way, I simply press the Tab key to hide the palettes and get them out of the way.

The other advantage of never moving the palettes is that if I do actually close a palette or palettes, I always know where a given palette is going to be when I reopen it and don't have to waste time looking for it.

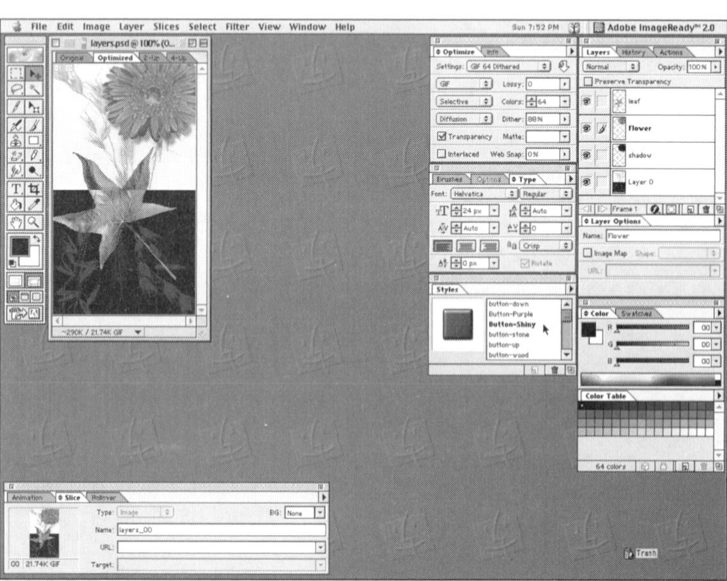

Show or Hide All Palettes

Both: Tab

Show or Hide All But the Tool Palette

Both: Shift+Tab

Remove the Focus of a Numeric Edit Field in a Palette

Both: Enter or Return

Show or Hide the Optimize Palette

Menu: Window→Show/Hide Optimize

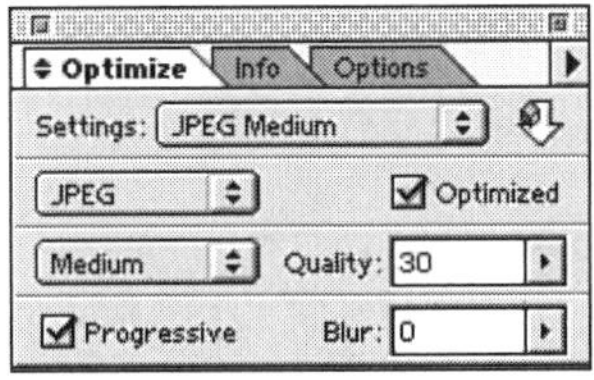

Show or Hide the Info Palette

Menu: Window→Show/Hide Info

Both: F8

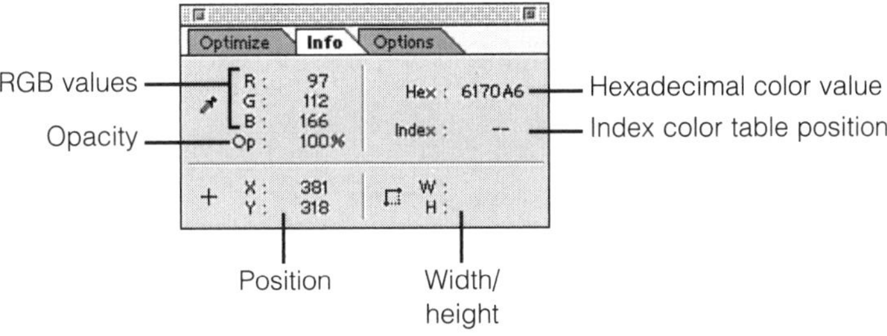

Open the Options Palette

Menu: Window→Show/Hide Options

Both: Enter or Return

Mouse: Double-click on a tool

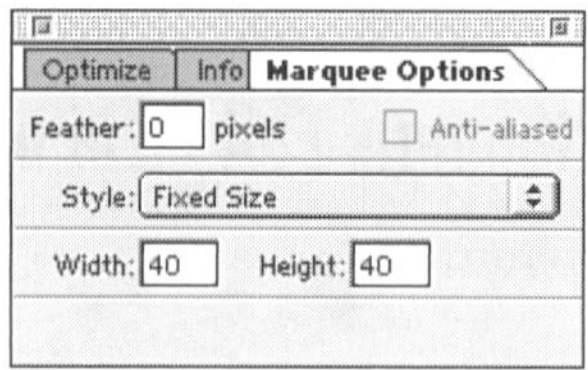

Show or Hide the Color Palette

Menu: Window→Show/Hide Color

Both: F6

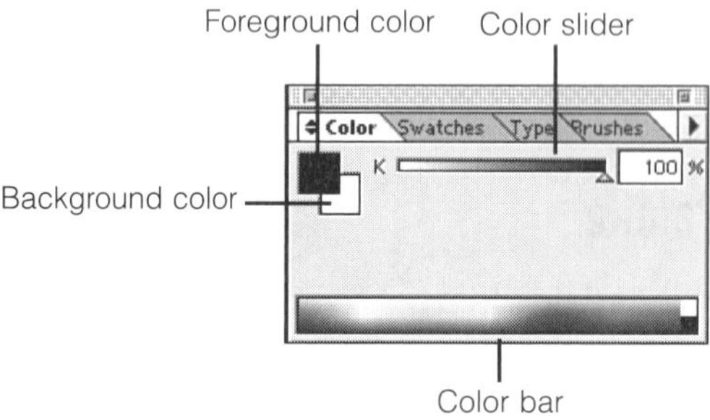

Select Background Color (in the Color Palette)

Mac: Option-Click on color ramp

Win: Alt+Click on color ramp

Cycle Through Color Ramps in the Color Palette

Both: Shift+Click on color bar

The default color bar at the bottom of the Color palette displays the RGB color spectrum for quick selection of colors without having to open the Color Picker dialog box. You can change the ramp to display an RGB, CMYK, Grayscale, or Current Colors color ramp.

Choose a Specific Color Bar

Mac: Ctrl-Click on color bar

Win: Right-click on color bar

This displays a contextual menu of the four different display choices for the color bar, plus the option to choose Make Ramp Web Safe.

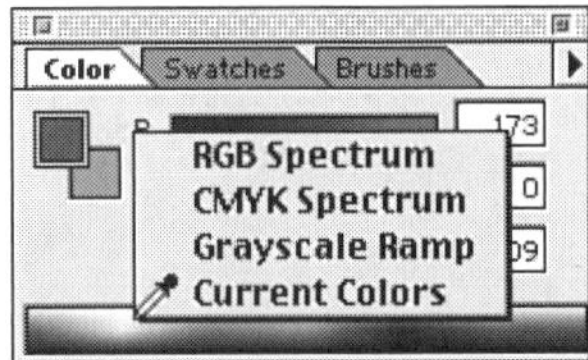

Show or Hide the Swatches Palette

Menu: Window→Show/Hide Swatches

Both: F6

F6 shows or hides the Color palette. Also use it to show or hide the Swatches palette. To show Swatches if the Color palette is not open, press F6, and then click the Swatches tab. To hide both the Swatches and the Color palettes, press the F6 key until they both disappear.

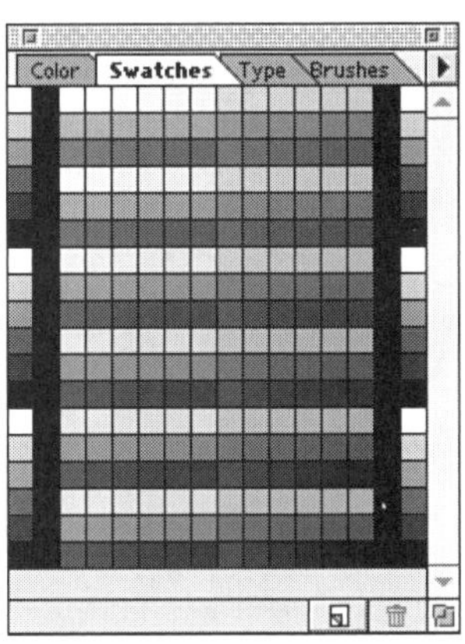

Add Foreground Color as a New Swatch

Mouse: Click on an empty slot in the Swatches palette

Look for the cursor to change into a bucket icon.

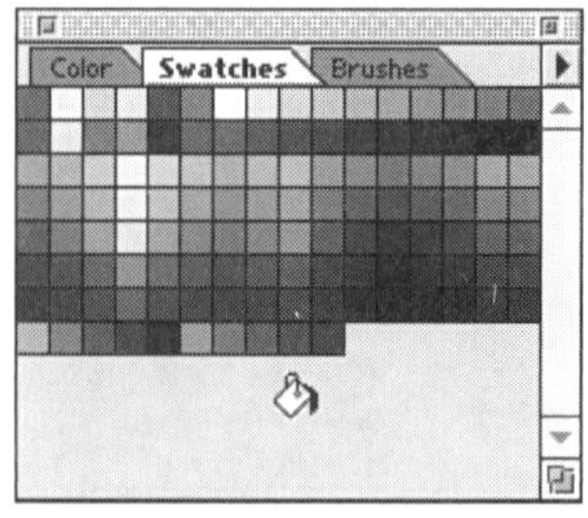

Delete a Swatch

Mac: Cmd-Click on a swatch

Win: Ctrl+Click on a swatch

Look for the cursor to change into a scissors icon.

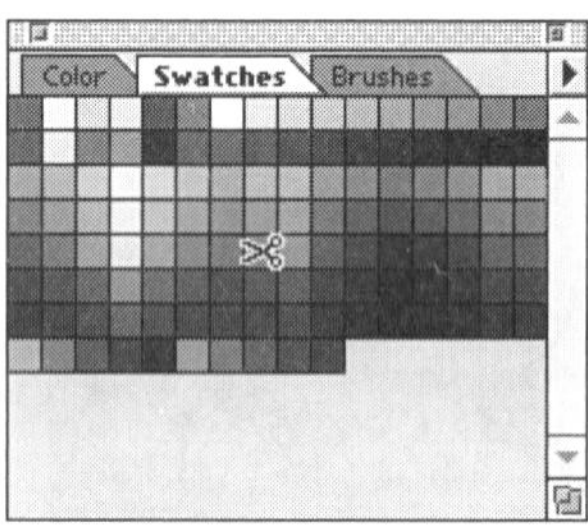

Insert Foreground Color as a New Swatch

Mac: Option-Shift-Click in the palette

Win: Alt+Shift+Click in the palette

This inserts a swatch of the current foreground color and shifts the rest of the swatches in the palette to the right.

Replace a Swatch with the Foreground Color

Both: Shift+Click on a swatch

Choose a Swatch for the Foreground Color

Mouse: Click on a swatch

Choose a Swatch for the Background Color

Mac: Option-Click on a swatch

Win: Alt+Click on a swatch

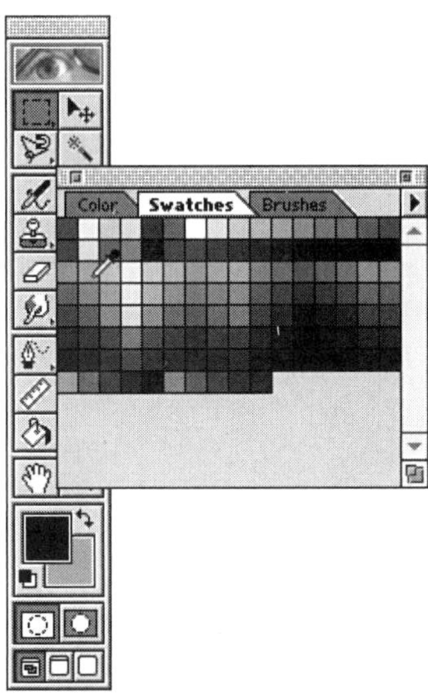

Show or Hide the Type Palette

Menu: Window→Show/Hide Type

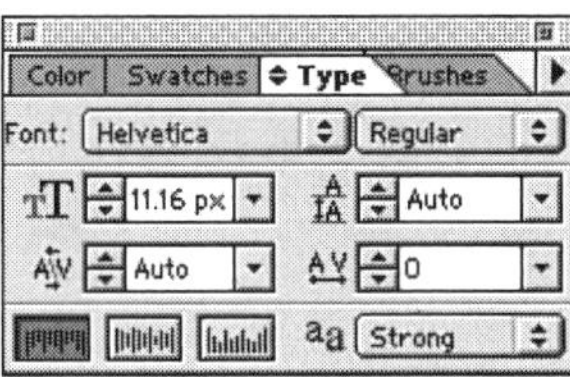

Show or Hide the Brushes Palette

Menu: Window→Show/Hide Brushes

Both: F5

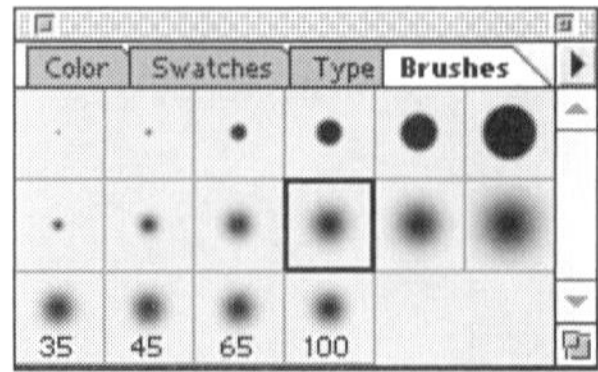

Show or Hide the Color Table

Menu: Window→Show/Hide Color Table

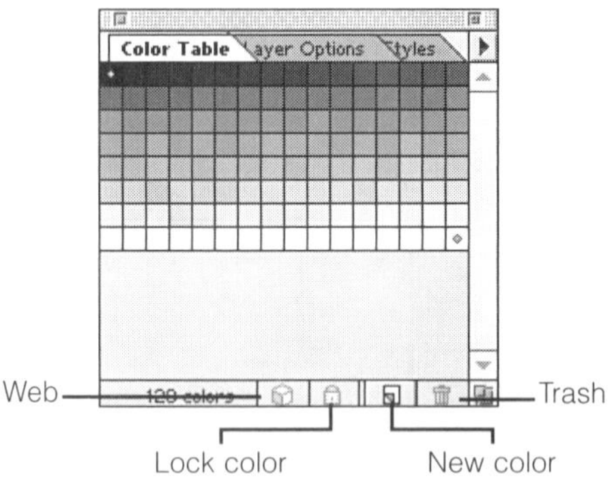

Select Multiple Contiguous Colors

Mouse: Shift+Click a second color

Click the first color to select it. Shift+clicking a second color selects all the colors in-between the two colors. The second color you click becomes the current foreground color.

Select Multiple Discontiguous Colors

Mac: Cmd-Click a swatch

Win: Ctrl+Click a swatch

The last color you clicked becomes the current foreground color.

Add Current Background Color to the Color Table

Mac: Option-Click the New Color button

Win: Alt+Click the New Color button

You can also drag the background color proxy from the Tool palette to the New Color button on the Color Table palette.

Show or Hide the Layer Options/Effects Palette

Menu: Window→Show/Hide Layer Options/Effects

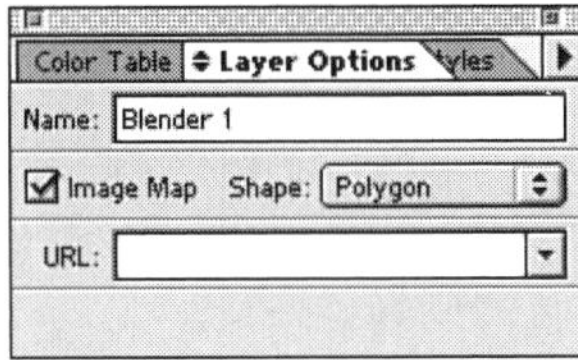

Show or Hide the Styles Palette

Menu: Window→Show/Hide Styles

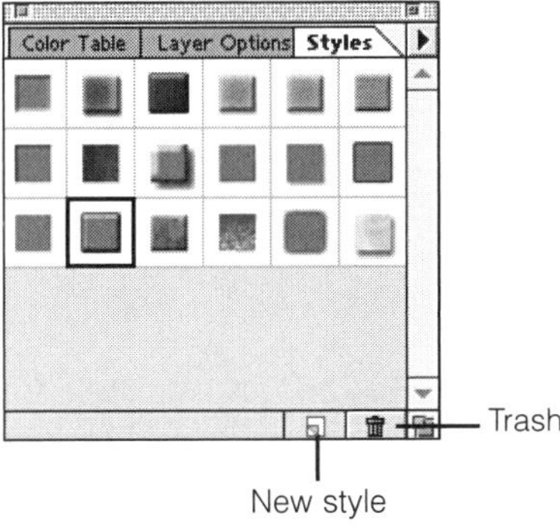

Show or Hide the Layers Palette

Menu: Window→Show/Hide Layers

Both: F7

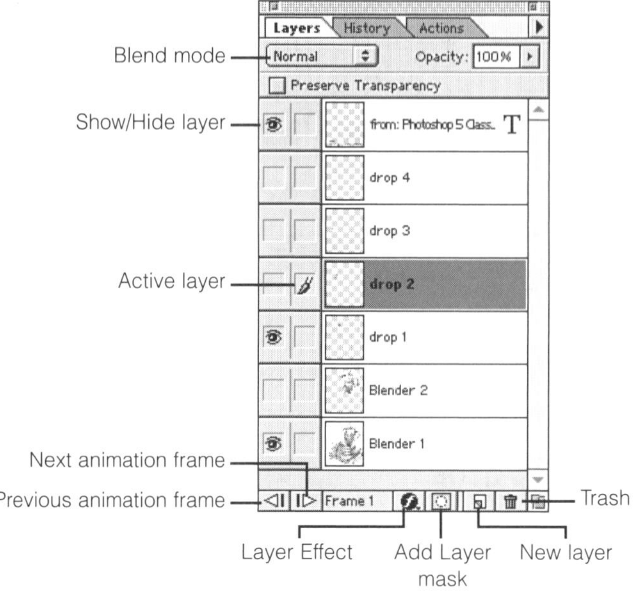

Show or Hide the History Palette

Menu: Window→Show/Hide History

Both: F9

F9 shows or hides the Actions palette. Also use it to show or hide the History palette. To show History if the Actions palette is not open, press F9, and then click on the History tab. To hide both the History and the Actions palettes, press the F9 key until they both disappear.

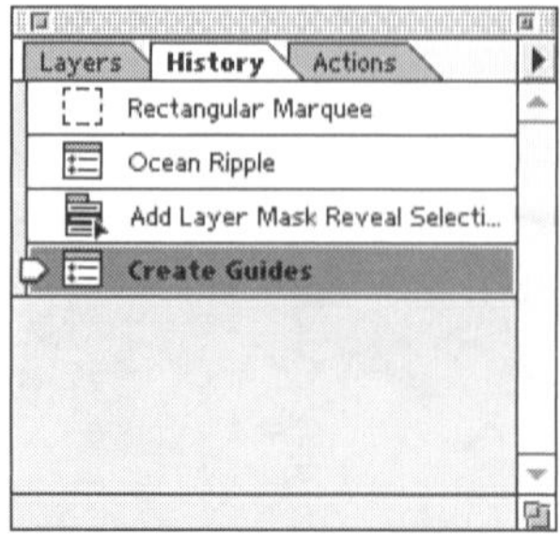

Step Backward (Multiple Undo)

Menu: History→Step Backward

Mac: Cmd-Option-Z

Win: Ctrl+Alt+Z

Step Forward (Multiple Redo)

Menu: History→Step Forward

Mac: Cmd-Shift-Z

Win: Ctrl+Shift+Z

Show or Hide the Actions Palette

Menu: Window→Show/Hide Actions

Both: F9

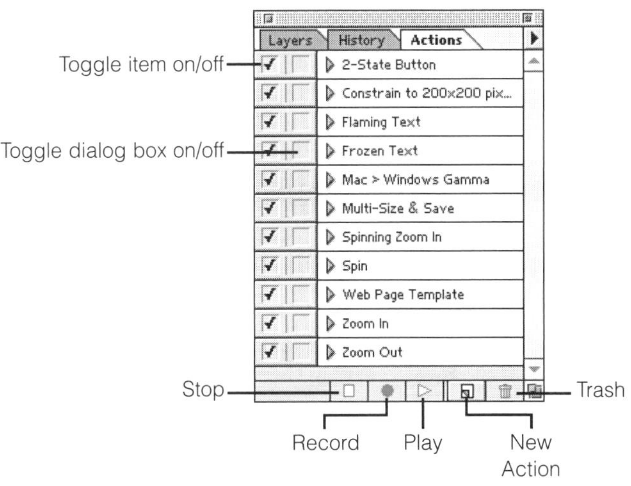

Show or Hide the Animation Palette

Menu: Window→Show/Hide Animation

Both: F11

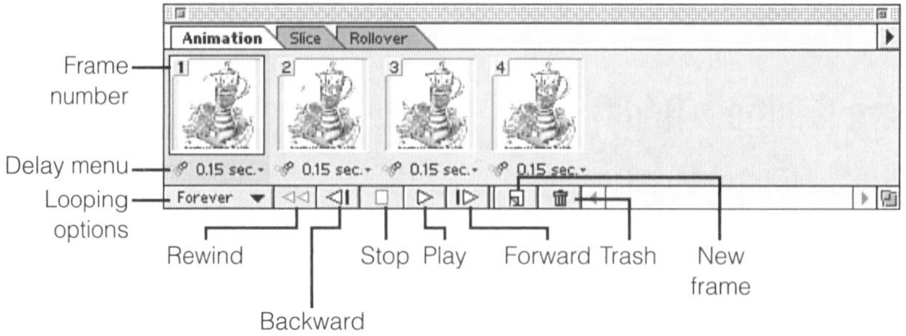

Select/Deselect Multiple Contiguous Frames

Mouse: Shift+Click a frame

Select/Deselect Multiple Discontiguous Frames

Mac: Cmd-Click a frame

Win: Ctrl+Click a frame

Insert Pasted Frame After the Current Frame

Both: Shift+Paste Frame

Normally, choosing Paste Frame from the Animation palette options menu adds the contents of the copied frame to the contents of the current frame. Holding down Shift inserts the copied contents into a new frame inserted after the current frame.

Duplicate the Layers Used in the Current Frame in the Layers Palette

Mac: Cmd-Paste Frame

Win: Ctrl+Paste Frame

Normally, choosing Paste Frame from the Animation palette options menu adds the contents of the copied frame to the contents of the current frame. Holding down (Cmd) [Ctrl] duplicates the layers used in the frame in the Layers palette. It also includes the duplicated layers in the current frame.

Duplicate the Layers Used in the Current Frame in the Layers Palette and Insert Pasted Frame After the Current Frame

Mac: Cmd-Shift-Paste Frame

Win: Ctrl+Shift+Paste Frame

Normally, choosing Paste Frame from the Animation palette options menu adds the contents of the copied frame to the contents of the current frame. Holding down (Cmd-Shift) [Ctrl+Shift] keys duplicates the layers used in the frame in the Layers palette. Also, rather than including the duplicated layers in the current frame, it inserts the copied contents into a new frame inserted after the current frame.

Replace the Destination Frame with the Copied Frame(s)

Mac: Option-Shift-Paste Frame

Win: Alt+Shift+Paste Frame

Normally, choosing Paste Frame from the Animation palette options menu adds the contents of the copied frame to the contents of the current frame. Holding down the (Option-Shift) [Alt+Shift] keys replaces the contents of the destination frame with the contents of the copied frame(s).

Show or Hide the Slice Palette

Menu: Window→Show/Hide Slice

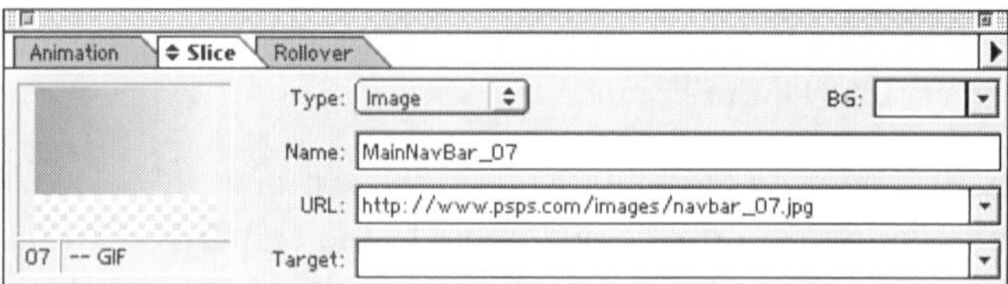

Move the Contents of the Selected Layer Concurrently in All Selected Animation Frames

Mac: Cmd-Shift-Drag with the Move tool

Win: Ctrl+Shift+Drag with the Move tool

Tools

Tool Shortcuts

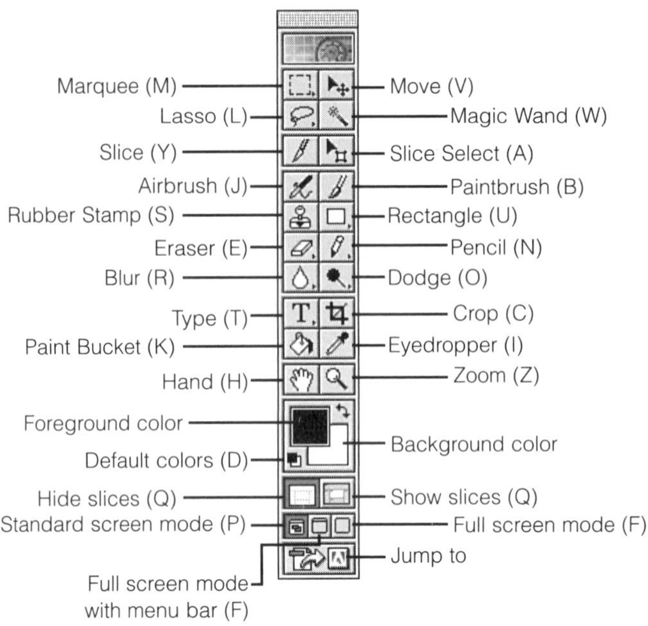

Cycle Through the Available Tools in a Tool Slot

Mac: Option-Click on tool slot

Win: Alt+Click on tool slot

If you use the mouse to switch from tool to tool rather than using the keystroke assigned to each tool, you can avoid using the tool slot flyouts to switch to a tool that you can't see by (Option) [Alt] clicking on the tool slot. Keep clicking on the tool slot until you switch to the tool you want.

Cycle Through Marquee Tools

Both: Shift+M

This toggles you back and forth between the Rectangular Marquee, Rounded Rectangle Marquee, Elliptical Marquee, Single Row Marquee, and Single Column Marquee tools.

Toggle to the Move Tool

Mac: Cmd

Win: Ctrl

This allows you to temporarily switch to the Move tool while any other tool is selected.

Move Selection Marquee 1 Pixel

Both: Arrow keys

Mouse: With a selection tool active, place cursor inside the selection, then press and drag

As long as a selection tool is active (Marquee, Lasso, Magic Wand), the arrow keys move just the selection marquee—not any pixels—one pixel in the direction of the arrow key you choose.

Move Selection Marquee 10 Pixels

Both: Shift+Arrow keys

Mouse: With a selection tool active, place cursor inside the selection, then press and drag

As long as a selection tool is active (Marquee, Lasso, Magic Wand), holding down the Shift key and then using the arrow keys moves a selection marquee 10 pixels in the direction of the arrow key you choose.

Move Selected Pixels 1 Pixel

Menu: Edit→Transform→Numeric

Both: Arrow keys

Mouse: With the Move tool active, press and drag

As long as the Move tool is active, the arrow keys move selected pixels one pixel in the direction of the arrow key you choose. If any other tool is active, hold down the (Cmd) [Ctrl] key, and then use the arrow keys.

Move Selected Pixels 10 Pixels

Menu: Edit→Transform→Numeric

Both: Shift+Arrow keys

Mouse: With the Move tool active, press and drag

As long as the Move tool is active, holding down the Shift key and then pressing the arrow keys moves selected pixels 10 pixels in the direction of the arrow key you choose. If any other tool is active, hold down the (Cmd-Shift) [Ctrl+Shift] keys, and then use the arrow keys.

Select a Layer by Name

Mac: Ctrl-Click

Win: Right-click

This shortcut will display a pop-up menu that lists all the available layers directly under the cursor, as long as a layer actually has some pixels under the cursor. Simply choose the layer you want from the list. This shortcut illustrates the need for you to always name your layers something relevant rather than using the default names of Layer 1, Layer 2, and so on.

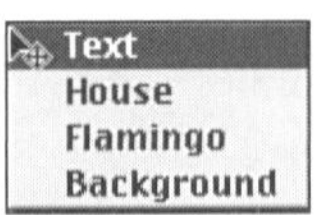

Select the Top-Most Visible Layer

Mac: Ctrl-Option-Click

Win: Alt+Right-click

This shortcut will select the top-most layer directly under the cursor.

Draw Using the Polygonal Lasso Tool

Mac: Option-Click/Drag

Win: Alt+Click/Drag

This shortcut allows you to temporarily switch to the Polygonal Lasso tool while using the regular Lasso tool.

Cycle Through Lasso Tools

Both: Shift+L

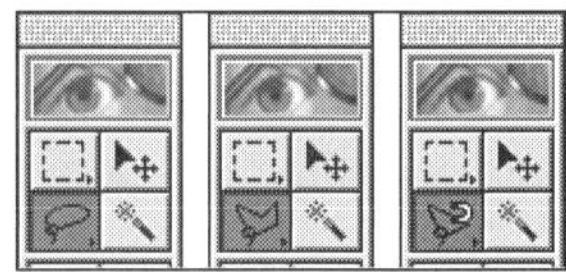

Draw Using the Lasso Tool

Mac: Option-Click/Drag

Win: Alt+Click/Drag

This shortcut allows you to temporarily switch to the Lasso tool while using the Polygonal Lasso tool.

Slice Tool

Both: Y

Slice Select Tool

Both: A

Specify Clone Source

Mac: Option-Click

Win: Alt+Click

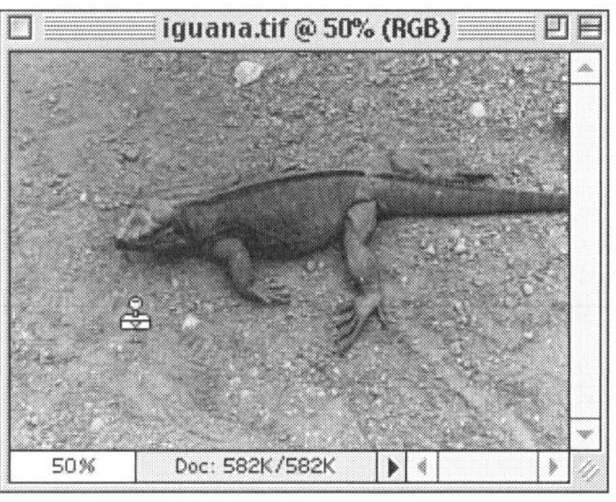

Rectangle Tool

VERSION 2.0

Both: U

This tool is a shortcut in and of itself—it eliminates the need to create a new layer, use a selection tool to create a selected area, and then fill the area with color using a fill command by doing all of these steps for you.

Cycle Through the Rectangle, Rounded Rectangle, and Ellipse Tools

VERSION 2.0

Both: Shift+U

These tools are a shortcuts themselves—they eliminate the need to create a new layer, use a selection tool to create a selected area, and then fill the area with color using a fill command by doing all of these steps for you.

Cycle Through Eraser Tools

Both: Shift+E

This toggles you back and forth between the Eraser and the Magic Eraser tools. Note: There is no Background Eraser in ImageReady.

Cycle Through Pencil and Line Tools

Both: Shift+N

Cycle Through Blur, Sharpen, and Smudge Tools

Both: Shift+R

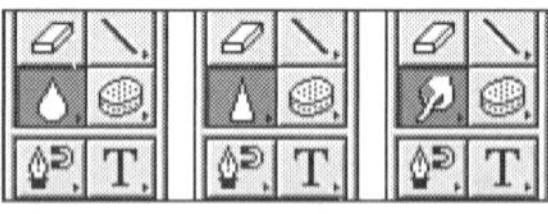

Toggle to the Blur Tool

Mac: Option

Win: Alt

Toggle to the Sharpen Tool

Mac: Option

Win: Alt

Smudge Using Foreground Color

Mac: Option

Win: Alt

Cycle Through Toning Tools

Both: Shift+O

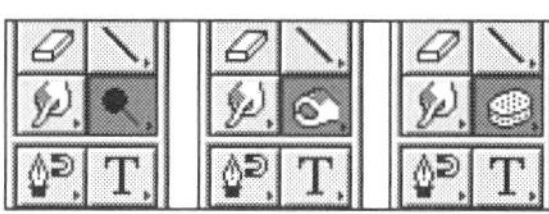

Toggle to the Dodge Tool

Mac: Option

Win: Alt

Toggle to the Burn Tool

Mac: Option

Win: Alt

Set Dodge Tool to Affect Shadows

Mac: Option-Shift-W

Win: Alt+Shift+W

Set Dodge Tool to Affect Midtones

Mac: Option-Shift-V

Win: Alt+Shift+V

Set Dodge Tool to Affect Highlights

Mac: Option-Shift-Z

Win: Alt+Shift+Z

Set Burn Tool to Affect Shadows

Mac: Option-Shift-W

Win: Alt+Shift+W

Set Burn Tool to Affect Midtones

Mac: Option-Shift-V

Win: Alt+Shift+V

Set Burn Tool to Affect Highlights

Mac: Option-Shift-Z

Win: Alt+Shift+Z

Set Sponge Tool to Desaturate

Mac: Option-Shift-J

Win: Alt+Shift+J

Set Sponge Tool to Saturate

Mac: Option-Shift-A

Win: Alt+Shift+A

Cycle Through Type Tools

Both: Shift+T

Changing the Canvas Color

Mouse: Shift+Click on the canvas with the Bucket tool

To change the canvas color from the default gray to the current foreground color, hold down the Shift key and click on the canvas with the Bucket tool. Mostly, this is a great practical joke to play on a co-worker when he mistakenly leaves Photoshop open on his machine when he goes to lunch. Then you come in and change the canvas color to toxic green. However, there is a practical reason to know about this shortcut: If you will be printing the image, it allows you to simulate what your image looks like against the color of the paper or background it will be printed on.

Cycle Through Eyedropper Tools

Both: Shift+I

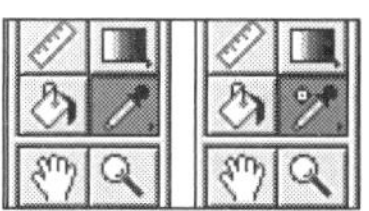

Toggle to the Eyedropper Tool

Mac: Option

Win: Alt

Hold down the specified key to temporarily switch to the Eyedropper tool so that you can choose a new foreground color. This shortcut works when using any of the following tools: Airbrush, Paintbrush, Gradient, Paint Bucket, Pencil, and Line.

Select Background Color When Using the Eyedropper Tool

Mac: Option-Click

Win: Alt+Click

Toggle to the Zoom Out Tool

Mac: Option-Spacebar

Win: Alt+Spacebar

Toggle to the Zoom In Tool

Mac: Cmd-Spacebar

Win: Ctrl+Spacebar

Zoom In

Menu: View→Zoom In

Mac: Cmd-+ (plus)

Win: Ctrl++ (plus)

Mouse: Click with the Zoom (Magnifying Glass) tool

Zoom Out

Menu: View→Zoom Out

Mac: Cmd-- (minus)

Win: Ctrl+- (minus)

Both: (Option+Click) with the Zoom (Magnifying Glass) tool; [Alt+Click] with the Zoom (Magnifying Glass) tool

Exchange Foreground and Background Colors

Both: X

Mouse: Click on curved double arrow in the Tools palette

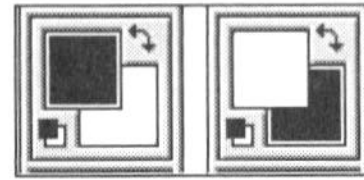

Reset Colors Back to Defaults

Both: D

Mouse: Click on miniature foreground/background icon in Tools palette

Toggle Show Slices

Both: Q

Toggle Screen Modes

Both: F

File
Edit
Image
Layer
Select
Filter
View
Window
Help
9:44 AM

Toggle to Menus While in Full Screen Mode

Both: Shift+F

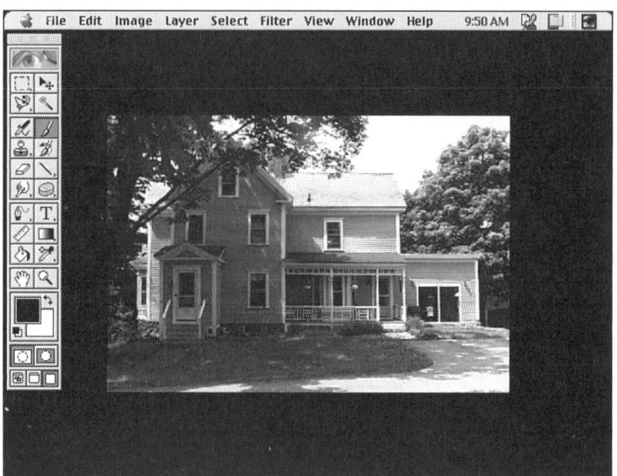

Cropping Shortcuts

Crop Tool

Both: C

Apply Crop

Both: Enter or Return

Cancel Crop

Mac: Cmd-. (period)

Win: Ctrl+. (period)

Both: Esc

Crop Without Snapping to Edges

Mac: Cmd-Drag

Win: Ctrl+Drag

Constrain Crop to a Square

Mouse: Shift+Drag handles

Resize Crop from the Center

Mac: Option-Drag handles

Win: Alt+Drag handles

Constrain Crop from the Center

Mac: Option-Shift-Drag handles

Win: Alt+Shift+Drag handles

Rotate the Cropping Boundary

Mouse: Drag outside the cropping box

Move the Cropping Box

Mouse: Drag inside the cropping box

Resize the Cropping Box

Mouse: Drag cropping box handles

Add Canvas to Image with the Crop Tool

Mouse: Resize cropping box beyond image area

This is another one of those cool hidden shortcuts because it isn't obvious at first. First, select the entire image area with the Crop tool. After you see the cropping box handles, you can then resize the box beyond the image area. When you apply the crop, it adds the additional canvas to the image area. To add canvas equally from the center of the image, hold down the (Option) [Alt] key while dragging a handle. Remember, you have to create a crop area first, and then you can adjust it outside the image area.

Painting Shortcuts

Select the Next Brush

Both:]

Select the Previous Brush

Both: [

Select the First Brush

Both: Shift+[

Select the Last Brush

Both: Shift+]

Create a New Brush

Both: Click in empty slot

Delete a Brush

Mac: Cmd-Click on the brush

Win: Ctrl+Click on the brush

Look for the cursor to change to a scissors icon.

Edit a Brush

Mouse: Double-click on the brush

Change Painting Tool Opacity in 1% Increments

Both: Type two numbers quickly (11=11%, 63=63%, and so on)

Change Painting Tool Opacity in 10% Increments

Both: Type a single number (1=10%, 2=20%, and so on)

Paint Constrained to Horizontal or Vertical Axis

Mouse: Shift+Drag

This shortcut works when using any of the following tools: Airbrush, Paintbrush, Rubber Stamp, Pattern Stamp, History Brush, Eraser, Pencil, Line, Blur, Sharpen, Smudge, Dodge, Burn, Sponge, and Gradient.

Paint or Draw in a Straight Line

Mouse: Shift+Click

This shortcut works when using any of the following tools: Airbrush, Paintbrush, Rubber Stamp, Pattern Stamp, History Brush, Eraser, Pencil, Pen, Line, Blur, Sharpen, Smudge, Dodge, Burn, Sponge, and Gradient.

Selection Tool Shortcuts

Constrain to a Square Selection

Mouse: Shift+Drag

This shortcut only works if you are starting a new selection. If a selection already exists, you will add to the selection instead.

Constrain to a Circle Selection

Mouse: Shift+Drag

This shortcut only works if you are starting a new selection. If a selection already exists, you will add to the selection instead.

Draw from the Center While Creating Selections

Mac: Option-Drag

Win: Alt+Drag

Normally, when creating a selection, the selection anchors itself from wherever you click, creating the selection outward from that position in a diagonal direction. With this shortcut, wherever you click becomes the center of the selection as you create it. Also, remember that this shortcut only works if you are starting a new selection. If a selection already exists, you will subtract from the selection instead.

Constrain and Draw from the Center While Creating Selections

Mac: Option-Shift-Drag

Win: Alt+Shift+Drag

Normally, when creating a selection, the selection anchors itself from wherever you click, creating the selection outward from that position in a diagonal direction. With this shortcut, wherever you click becomes the center of the selection as you create it. Also, remember that this shortcut only works if you are starting a new selection. If a selection already exists, you are left with the intersection of the selections instead.

Reposition a Selection as You Create It

Both: Spacebar

This is one of my favorite shortcuts. Sometimes you are trying to select a specific shape in an image and halfway through dragging out the selection, you realize you didn't start in the right position. Rather than starting over, just hold down the Spacebar. This allows you to drag the marquee to a different position. When you are ready to continue with the selection, just let go of the Spacebar. Remember to keep the mouse button down until you are finished making the selection.

Constrain a Selection as You Move It

Mouse: Shift+Drag

Make sure the cursor is within the selection area and that you press the mouse button down before you hold down the Shift key. If you hold down the Shift key first, you will add to the selection when you start dragging. If the cursor is outside the selected area, you will start a new selection instead of moving the existing one.

Register Items When Dragging from One Document to Another

Mouse: Shift+Drag from one document to the other

If you want the selection or layer from one document to end up in the same position in the target document you are dragging it to, make sure that they both have the same canvas size and hold down the Shift key as you drag the item to the target document. Let go of the mouse before letting go of the Shift key. Note: If the canvas sizes of the two documents are different, then holding down the Shift key places the dragged item in the center of the target document.

Duplicate a Selection

Mac: Option-Drag

Win: Alt+Drag

Add to a Selection

Mouse: Shift+Drag

This shortcut is the same when using any of the selection tools: Rectangular Marquee, Elliptical Marquee, or any of the Lasso tools. To use this shortcut with the Magic Wand tool, click instead of dragging.

Subtract from a Selection

Mac: Option-Drag

Win: Alt+Drag

This shortcut is the same when using any of the selection tools: Rectangular Marquee, Elliptical Marquee, or any of the Lasso tools. To use this shortcut with the Magic Wand tool, click instead of dragging.

Intersect with a Selection

Mac: Option-Shift-Drag

Win: Alt+Shift+Drag

This shortcut is the same when using any of the selection tools: Rectangular Marquee, Elliptical Marquee, or any of the Lasso tools. To use this shortcut with the Magic Wand tool, click instead of dragging.

Navigation

Navigation Shortcuts

Open Help

Menu: Help→Help Topics

Mac: Help key

Win: F1

Pan the Image

Both: Spacebar+Drag

Mouse: Press and drag with the Hand tool

Zoom Commands

Toggle to Zoom In Tool

Mac: Cmd-Spacebar

Win: Ctrl+Spacebar

Toggle to Zoom In Tool

Mac: Cmd

Win: Ctrl

This shortcut is only available when the Hand tool is the active tool—if you have either clicked on the Hand tool or typed "H".

Toggle to Zoom Out Tool

Mac: Option-Spacebar

Win: Alt+Spacebar

Toggle to Zoom Out Tool

Mac: Option

Win: Alt

This shortcut is only available when the Hand tool is the active tool—if you have either clicked on the Hand tool or typed "H".

Zoom In

Menu: View→Zoom In

Mac: Cmd-+ (plus)

Win: Ctrl++ (plus)

Mouse: Click with the Zoom (Magnifying Glass) tool

Zoom Out

Menu: View→Zoom Out

Mac: Cmd-- (minus)

Win: Ctrl+- (minus)

Mouse: (Option-Click) [Alt+Click] with the Zoom (Magnifying Glass) tool

Zoom to 100%

Menu: View→Fit on Screen

Mac: Cmd-Option-0

Win: Ctrl+Alt+0

Mouse: Double-click on Zoom Tool

Zoom to Fit on Screen

Menu: View→Actual Pixels

Mac: Cmd-0

Win: Ctrl+0

Mouse: Double-click on Hand tool

This shortcut enlarges the window to fill as much space as the palettes leave it. Bonus tip: If you want to use the whole screen, and don't mind if the image falls behind the palettes, hide the palettes by pressing the Tab key before using this shortcut.

Zoom In Without Changing the Window Size

Mac: Cmd-Option-+ (plus)

Win: Ctrl+Alt++ (plus)

Zoom Out Without Changing the Window Size

Mac: Cmd-Option-- (minus)

Win: Ctrl+Alt+- (minus)

Scrolling Shortcuts

Scroll Up One Full Screen

Both: Page Up

Scroll Down One Full Screen

Both: Page Down

Scroll Up 10 Pixels

Both: Shift+Page Up

Scroll Down 10 Pixels

Both: Shift+Page Down

Scroll Right 10 Pixels

Mac: Cmd-Shift-Page Down

Win: Ctrl+Shift+Page Down

Scroll Left 10 Pixels

Mac: Cmd-Shift-Page Up

Win: Ctrl+Shift+Page Up

Scroll to Upper-Left Corner of the Image Window

Both: Home key

Power Tip: Spotting.

When you want to remove dust and spots from an image, these keyboard shortcuts come in very handy. Zoom up to the view you want to be in, usually 100%, and then press the Home key to begin in the upper-left corner of the image window. Use the appropriate shortcuts to scroll down a screen at time until you get to the bottom. After you get to the bottom, use the appropriate shortcut to scroll over one screen to the right, and then start scrolling up one screen at a time. Repeat this process until you end up in the lower-right corner of the image window. The advantage of using this method is that you are guaranteed not to miss any pixels in the image. Look at the Navigator palette to show you where you are in the image.

Scroll to Lower-Right Corner of the Image Window

Both: End key

Dialog Boxes

Dialog Box Shortcuts

Increase Numeric Entry Values by 1

Both: Up Arrow

This works with most dialog boxes, and sometimes edits the values by .1 rather than 1 if the values allow decimal increments (for example, Feather).

Increase Numeric Entry Values by 10

Both: Shift+Up Arrow

This works with most dialog boxes, and sometimes edits the values by 1 rather than 10 if the values allow decimal increments (for example, Feather).

Decrease Numeric Entry Values by 1

Both: Down Arrow

This works with most dialog boxes, and sometimes edits the values by .1 rather than 1 if the values allow decimal increments (for example, Feather).

Decrease Numeric Entry Values by 10

Both: Shift+Down Arrow

This works with most dialog boxes, and sometimes edits the values by 1 rather than 10 if the values allow decimal increments (for example, Feather).

Cancel a Pop-Up Slider

VERSION 5.0

Both: Esc

Apply an Edit to a Pop-Up Slider

VERSION 5.0

Both: Return or Enter

Toggle to Previous Setting While Editing in a Pop-Up Slider

VERSION 5.0

Mac: Press Option while holding the mouse down outside of a slider rectangle

Win: Press Alt while holding the mouse down outside of a slider rectangle

Cancel Any Dialog Box

Mac: Cmd-. (period)

Win: Ctrl+. (period)

Both: Esc

Activate Any Button in an Alert Dialog Box

Both: Type the first letter of the button (for example, D = Don't Save)

Reset All Settings in a Dialog Box Without Exiting

Mac: Hold down Option to change the Cancel button to a Reset button

Win: Hold down Alt to change the Cancel button to a Reset button

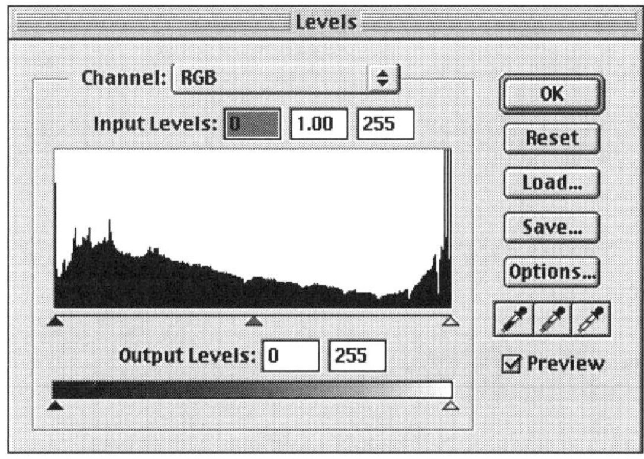

Pan Image While in a Dialog Box

Both: Spacebar+Drag

Zoom In While in a Dialog Box

Mac: Cmd-Click or Drag or Cmd-+ (plus)

Win: Ctrl+Click or Drag or Ctrl++ (plus)

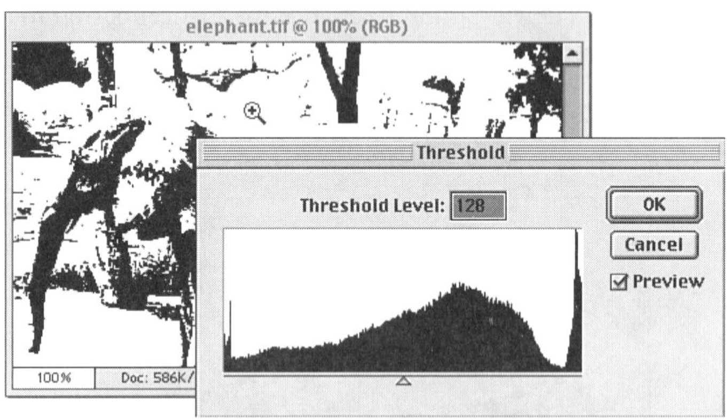

Zoom Out While in a Dialog Box

Mac: Option-Click or Drag or Cmd-- (minus)

Win: Alt+Click or Drag or Ctrl+- (minus)

The **File** Menu

File Commands

New

Menu: File→New

Mac: Cmd-N

Win: Ctrl+N

Create New File and Skip the New Dialog Box

Mac: Cmd-Shift-N

Win: Ctrl+Shift+N

This creates a new document matching the dimensions of the current Clipboard contents.

Open

Menu: File→Open

Mac: Cmd-O

Win: Ctrl+O

Close

Menu: File→Close

Mac: Cmd-W

Win: Ctrl+W

Close All Documents

Menu: Window→Close All

Mac: Cmd-Shift-W

Win: Ctrl+Shift+W

Revert

Menu: File→Revert

Both: F12

Save Optimized

Menu: File→Save Optimized

Mac: Cmd-Option-S

Win: Ctrl+Alt+S

Save Optimized As

Menu: File→Save Optimized As

Mac: Cmd-Option-Shift-S

Win: Ctrl+Alt+Shift+S

Save

Menu: File→Save

Mac: Cmd-S

Win: Ctrl+S

Save As

Menu: File→Save As

Mac: Cmd-Shift-S

Win: Ctrl+Shift+S

Quit

Menu: File→Quit

Mac: Cmd-Q

Win: Ctrl+Q

Image Info

Menu: File→Image Info

Mac: Cmd-Shift-K

Win: Ctrl+Shift+K

Preview in [Default] Browser

Menu: File→Preview In→[Default Browser]

Mac: Cmd-Option-P

Win: Ctrl+Alt+P

Jump To [Adobe Photoshop 5.5]

Menu: File→Jump To→Adobe Photoshop 5.5

Mac: Cmd-Shift-M

Win: Ctrl+Shift+M

Preferences

Toggle Precise Cursors

Menu: File→Preferences→Display & Cursors

Both: Caps Lock

Precise Cursors changes the display of the current tool into a cross-hair target. The Caps Lock key allows you to toggle this setting, regardless of the Display & Cursors setting in the Preferences dialog box.

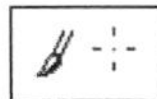

Preferences

Menu: File→Preferences

Mac: Cmd-K

Win: Ctrl+K

Reopen the Last Option Panel Used in Preferences

Menu: File→Preferences

Mac: Cmd-Option-K

Win: Ctrl+Alt+K

The **Edit** Menu

Edit Commands

Undo

Menu: Edit→Undo

Mac: Cmd-Z

Win: Ctrl+Z

Redo

Menu: Edit→Redo

Mac: Cmd-Z

Win: Ctrl+Z

Toggle Undo/Redo the Last Step

Menu: Edit→Undo/Redo

Mac: Cmd-Z

Win: Ctrl+Z

Cut

Menu: Edit→Cut

Mac: Cmd-X

Win: Ctrl+X

Copy

Menu: Edit→Copy

Mac: Cmd-C

Win: Ctrl+C

Copy Merged

Menu: Edit→Copy Merged

Mac: Cmd-Shift-C

Win: Ctrl+Shift+C

Paste

Menu: Edit→Paste

Mac: Cmd-V

Win: Ctrl+V

Copy HTML Code for Selected Slices

Menu: Edit→Copy HTML Code→Copy Selected Slices

Mac: Cmd-Option-C

Win: Ctrl+Alt+C

Fill Commands

Open the Fill Dialog Box

Menu: Edit→Fill

Mac: Shift-Delete

Win: Shift+Backspace

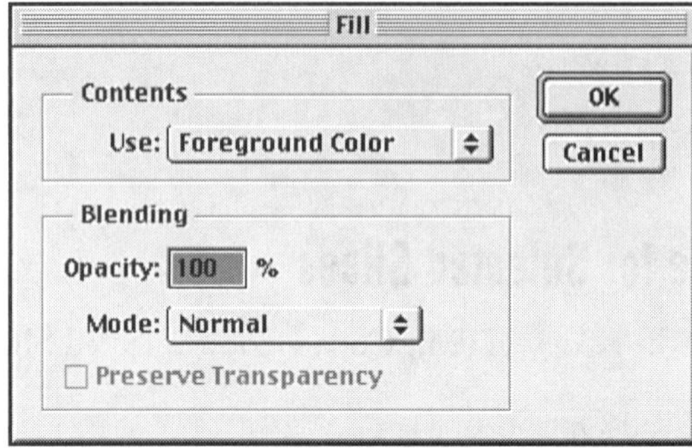

Fill with the Foreground Color

Menu: Edit→Fill

Mac: Option-Delete

Win: Alt+Backspace

Mouse: Bucket tool

This command fills the entire contents of the active layer or selection with the foreground color, unless the Preserve Transparency check box is turned on in the Layers palette.

Fill with the Foreground Color While Preserving Transparency

Menu: Edit→Fill

Mac: Option-Shift-Delete

Win: Alt+Shift+Backspace

This command only changes the color of the layer where there are actual pixels. All transparent areas are unchanged. This is an extremely efficient way to change the color of text on a Type layer. Note: Type layers always have Preserve Transparency turned on, so you CAN use the regular fill shortcuts. However, I recommend you remember this shortcut instead because it still works. That way, you only have to remember one shortcut for changing the color of type, whether it is a Type layer, or a Type layer that has been rendered.

Fill with the Background Color

Menu: Edit→Fill

Mac: Cmd-Delete

Win: Ctrl+Backspace

This command fills the entire contents of the active layer or selection with the background color.

Fill with the Background Color While Preserving Transparency

Menu: Edit→Fill

Mac: Cmd-Shift-Delete

Win: Ctrl+Shift+Backspace

This command only changes the color of the layer where there are actual pixels. All transparent areas are unchanged. This is an extremely efficient way to change the color of text on a Type layer. Note: Type layers always have Preserve Transparency turned on, so you CAN use the regular fill shortcuts. However, I recommend you remember this shortcut instead because it still works. That way, you only have to remember one shortcut for changing the color of type, whether it is a Type layer, or a Type layer that has been rendered.

Transformation Commands

Scale Using the Center Point

Mac: Option+Drag a corner handle

Win: Alt+Drag a corner handle

Skew Using the Center Point

Mac: Cmd-Option-Drag a middle handle

Win: Ctrl+Alt+Drag a middle handle

A middle handle means any of the non-corner handles.

Snap Angle Values to 15-Degree Increments

Mouse: Shift+Drag angle wheel

Apply Any Transformations

Both: Enter or Return

Cancel Any Transformations

Mac: Cmd-. (period)

Win: Ctrl+. (period)

Both: Esc

Free Transform

Menu: Edit→Free Transform

Mac: Cmd-T

Win: Ctrl+T

Transform Again

Menu: Edit→Transform→Again

Mac: Cmd-Shift-T

Win: Ctrl+Shift+T

This shortcut repeats the last transformation settings you used.

Create a Duplicate While Transforming

Mac: Cmd+Option+T

Win: Ctrl+Alt+T

Create a Duplicate While Transforming Again

Mac: Cmd-Option-Shift-T

Win: Ctrl+Alt+Shift+T

This shortcut creates a duplicate and repeats the last transformation settings you used.

Skew Using the Center Point and Constrain the Axis

Mac: Cmd-Option-Shift-Drag a middle handle

Win: Ctrl+Alt+Shift+Drag a middle handle

A middle handle means any of the non-corner handles.

The **Image** Menu

Image Adjustment Commands

Levels

Menu: Image→Adjust→Levels

Mac: Cmd-L

Win: Ctrl+L

Auto Levels

Menu: Image→Adjust→Auto Levels

Mac: Cmd-Shift-L

Win: Ctrl+Shift+L

Auto Contrast

Menu: Image→Adjust→Auto Contrast

Mac: Cmd-Option-Shift-L

Win: Ctrl+Alt+Shift+L

Hue/Saturation

Menu: Image→Adjust→Hue/Saturation

Mac: Cmd-U

Win: Ctrl+U

Desaturate Image

Menu: Image→Adjust→Desaturate

Mac: Cmd-Shift-U

Win: Ctrl+Shift+U

Invert

Menu: Image→Adjust→Invert

Mac: Cmd-I

Win: Ctrl+I

Cropping

Apply Crop

Both: Enter or Return

Cancel Crop

Mac: Cmd-. (period)

Win: Ctrl+. (period)

Both: Esc

Rotate the Cropping Boundary

Mouse: Drag outside the cropping box

Move the Cropping Box

Mouse: Drag inside the cropping box

Resize the Cropping Box

Mouse: Drag cropping box handles

Add Canvas to Image with the Crop Tool

Mouse: Resize cropping box beyond image area

This is another one of those cool hidden shortcuts because it isn't obvious at first. First, select the entire image area with the Crop tool. After you see the cropping box handles, you can then resize the box beyond the image area. When you apply the crop, it adds the additional canvas to the image area. To add canvas equally from the center of the image, hold down the (Option) [Alt] key while dragging a handle. Remember, you have to create a crop area first, and then you can adjust it outside the image area.

Constrain Crop to a Square

Mouse: Shift+Drag handles

Resize Crop from the Center

Mac: Option-Drag handles

Win: Alt+Drag handles

Constrain Crop from the Center

Mac: Option-Shift-Drag handles

Win: Alt+Shift+Drag handles

Crop Without Snapping to Edges

Mac: Cmd-Drag

Win: Ctrl+Drag

The **Layers** Menu

Creating and Deleting Layers

Create a New Layer with the New Layer Dialog Box

Menu: Layer→New→Layer

Mac: Option-Click on New Layer icon or Cmd-Shift-N

Win: Alt+Click on New Layer icon or Ctrl+Shift+N

This method presents the New Layer dialog box, giving you a chance to name the new layer and specify other options such as opacity and blend mode as you create the layer.

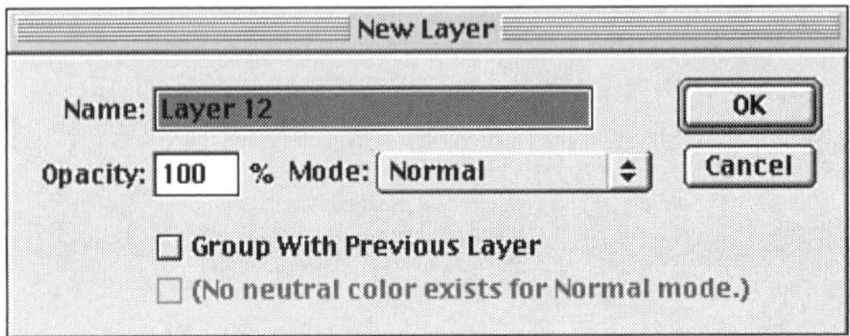

Create a New Layer and Bypass the New Layer Dialog Box

Menu: (Option)-Layer→New→Layer; [Alt]+Layer→New→Layer

Mac: Cmd-Option-Shift-N

Win: Ctrl+Alt+Shift+N

Mouse: Click the New Layer icon

This shortcut skips the New Layer dialog box when creating a new layer. Layers are named automatically (Layer 1, Layer 2, and so on). Just hold down the specified modifier key as you choose the menu command.

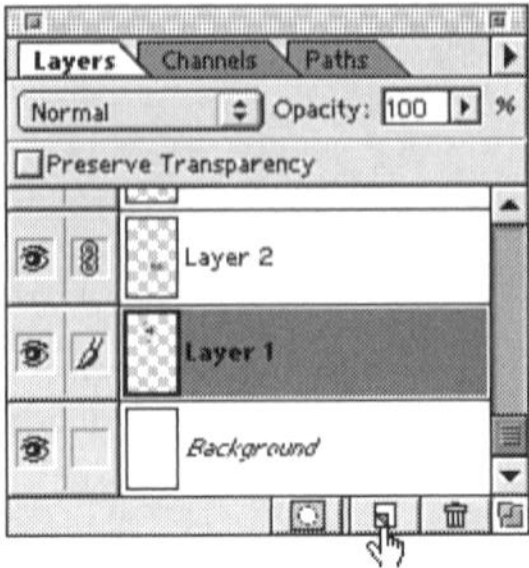

New Layer Via Copy

Menu: Layer→New→Layer Via Copy

Mac: Cmd-J

Win: Ctrl+J

New Layer Via Cut

Menu: Layer→New→Layer Via Cut

Mac: Cmd-Shift-J

Win: Ctrl+Shift+J

New Layer Via Copy with Make Layer Dialog Box

Menu: Layer→New→Layer Via Copy

Mac: Cmd-Option-J

Win: Ctrl+Alt+J

New Layer Via Cut with Make Layer Dialog Box

Menu: Layer→New→Layer Via Cut

Mac: Cmd-Option-Shift-J

Win: Ctrl+Option+Shift+J

Duplicate a Layer, Part 1

Mac: Cmd-A, Cmd-J

Win: Ctrl+A, Ctrl+J

Mouse: Drag the layer to the New Layer button

There is no single keyboard shortcut for duplicating an existing layer; however, there is a workaround. First, use the Select All command, and then use the Copy Selection into a New Layer command. This may seem kind of silly at first—why not just use the standard method of dragging the layer's name to the New Layer button? When you drag a layer to the New Layer button while recording an Action, the layer's actual name gets included in the Action. This can create problems when you want to play the Action back sometime in the future. For instance, if you dragged a layer named "Bob" to the New Layer button, the name "Bob" is included in the Action. The next time you play the Action, if there is not a layer named "Bob" in the current file, your Action will not work.

Duplicate a Layer, Part 2

Mac: Cmd-Option-Arrow key

Win: Ctrl+Alt+Arrow key

Mouse: Drag the layer to the New Layer button

Ok, I lied. There actually is a keyboard shortcut for duplicating an existing layer. However, there's a catch, so it is only a half-lie. This shortcut also moves the duplicated layer one pixel in the direction of the arrow key that you used. So, if you plan on moving the duplicated layer anyway, this is no big deal, and is a great shortcut. However, if you need the duplicated layer to be in the exact same position as the original, you will need to press the opposite arrow key once to get it back to the original position.

Note: If there is an active selection, this shortcut actually duplicates the selection and moves it on the target layer, not on a duplicate layer.

Delete a Layer

Mouse: Click the Delete Layer button

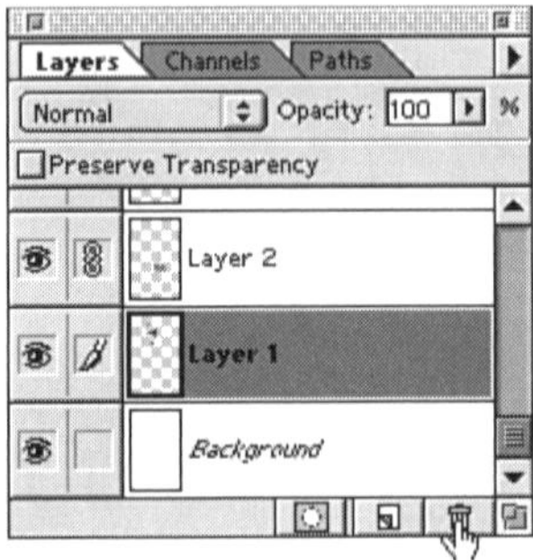

Delete a Layer and Skip the Warning Alert

Mac: Option-Click the Delete Layer button

Win: Alt+Click the Delete Layer button

Delete Multiple Layers

Both: Merge Visible, and then click the Delete Layer button

There is no way to select multiple layers to delete them all at once. However, there is a shortcut. First, hide all the layers you want to keep, and then use the Merge Visible shortcut to merge all the layers you want to delete into a single layer. Now, simply delete this single composite layer.

Selecting and Showing Layer Commands

Show or Hide a Layer

Mouse: Click in Eye icon area

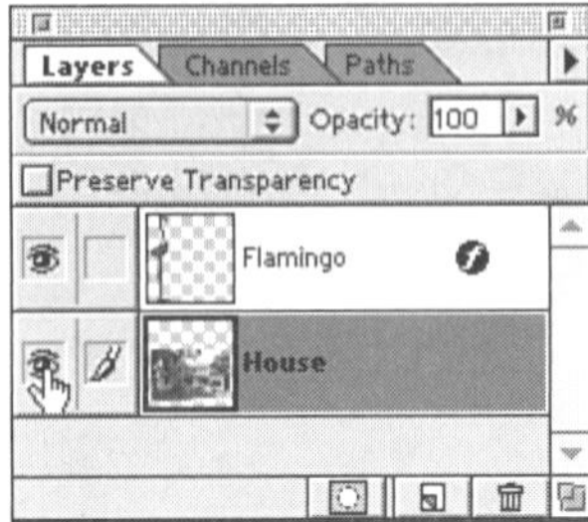

Show Just This Layer/Show All Layers

Mac: Option-Click in Eye icon area

Win: Alt+Click in Eye icon area

View and Select One Layer at a Time

Mac: Option-Click on layer name

Win: Alt+Click on layer name

This tip only works when only one layer is currently visible. In other words, hide all other layers except one, and then you can use this tip to simultaneously show the next layer you select and hide the previously shown layer. Note: There is a subtle difference here when clicking on the layer name versus clicking on the eyeball area. If you click on the eyeball area instead, the previous layer stays selected as the active layer, not the layer you just clicked the eyeball for.

Show/Hide Multiple Layers

Mouse: Drag through Eye icon area

Activate Next Visible Layer (Up)

Mac: Option-]

Win: Alt+]

Activate Previous Visible Layer (Down)

Mac: Option-[

Win: Alt+[

Activate the Bottom Layer

Mac: Option-Shift-[

Win: Alt+Shift+[

Activate the Top Layer

Mac: Option-Shift-]

Win: Alt+Shift+]

Select a Layer by Name

Mac: Ctrl-Click

Win: Right-click

This shortcut displays a pop-up menu that lists all the available layers directly under the cursor, as long as a layer actually has some pixels under the cursor. Simply choose the layer you want from the list. This shortcut illustrates the need for you to always name your layers something relevant rather than using the default names of Layer 1, Layer 2, and so on.

Select the Top-Most Visible Layer

Mac: Ctrl-Option-Click

Win: Alt+Right-click

This shortcut selects the top-most layer directly under the cursor.

Layer Editing Commands

Change Layer Opacity in 1% Increments

Both: Type two numbers quickly (11=11%, 63=63%, and so on)

This shortcut only works when you have a selection or the Move tool is the active tool. Otherwise, this shortcut changes the opacity of the active Painting tool.

Change Layer Opacity in 10% Increments

Both: Type a single number (1=10%, 2=20%, and so on)

This shortcut only works when you have a selection or the Move tool is the active tool. Otherwise, this shortcut changes the opacity of the active Painting tool.

Moving Layers

Move Layer 1 Pixel

Menu: Edit→Transform→Numeric

Both: Arrow keys

Mouse: With the Move tool active, press the mouse button and drag

As long as the Move tool is active, the arrow keys move a layer one pixel in the direction of the arrow key you choose. If any other tool is active, hold down the (Cmd) [Ctrl] key, and then use the arrow keys.

Move Layer 10 Pixels

Menu: Edit→Transform→Numeric

Both: Shift+Arrow keys

Mouse: With the Move tool active, press the mouse button and drag

As long as the Move tool is active, holding down the Shift key and then pressing the arrow keys moves a layer 10 pixels in the direction of the arrow key you choose. If any other tool is active, hold down the (Cmd-Shift) [Ctrl+Shift] keys, and then use the arrow keys.

Move Target Layer Up

Menu: Layer→Arrange→Bring Forward

Mac: Cmd-]

Win: Ctrl+]

Move Target Layer Down

Menu: Layer→Arrange→Send Backward

Mac: Cmd-[

Win: Ctrl+[

Move Target Layer to the Top

Menu: Layer→Arrange→Bring to Front

Mac: Cmd-Shift-]

Win: Ctrl+Shift+]

Move Target Layer to the Bottom

Menu: Layer→Arrange→Send to Back

Mac: Cmd-Shift-[

Win: Ctrl+Shift+[

Note, if there is a background layer in the file, the target layer stops above the background layer. To move a layer below the background layer, you must convert the background layer to a layer that supports transparency first.

Center When Dragging from One File to Another

Mouse: Shift+Drag from one document to the other

If you want the selection or layer from one document to end up in the middle of the document you are dragging it to, hold down the Shift key and drag the item to the target document. Let go of the mouse before letting go of the Shift key. Note: If the canvas sizes of the two documents are the same, then holding down the Shift key places the dragged item in the target document in the same position as the original document.

Register Items When Dragging from One Document to Another

Mouse: Shift+Drag from one document to the other

If you want the selection or layer from one document to end up in the same position in the target document you are dragging it to, make sure that they both have the same canvas size and hold down the Shift key as you drag the item to the target document. Let go of the mouse before letting go of the Shift key. Note: if the canvas sizes of the two documents are different, then holding down the Shift key places the dragged item in the center of the target document.

Linking and Grouping Shortcuts

Group Target Layer with the Previous Layer (Below)

Menu: Layer→Group with Previous

Mac: Cmd-G

Win: Ctrl+G

Ungroup Target Layer with the Previous Layer (Below)

Menu: Layer→Ungroup

Mac: Cmd-Shift-G

Win: Ctrl+Shift+G

Toggle Group/Ungroup with the Previous Layer

Mac: Option-Click on divider between layers

Win: Alt+Click on divider between layers

Layer Merging Commands

Merge Target Layer into the Layer Below

Menu: Layer→Merge Down

Mac: Cmd-E

Win: Ctrl+E

This command merges the target layer with the layer below it, as long as the layer below the target layer is visible. The name of the layer below the target layer is the name that is kept.

Merge All Visible Layers into the Target Layer

Menu: Layer→Merge Visible

Mac: Cmd-Shift-E

Win: Ctrl+Shift+E

This command merges all visible layers into the target layer. The name of the target layer is the name that is kept.

Merge a Copy of All Visible Layers into the Target Layer

Both: (Option)-Merge Visible; [Alt]+Merge Visible

Mac: Cmd-Option-Shift-E

Win: Ctrl+Alt+Shift+E

This command merges a copy of all the visible layers into the target layer, leaving the original layers intact. However, this does change the target layer. What you might want to do instead is to create a composite copy of all visible layers into a new layer. To accomplish this, just do the obvious: Create a new layer before using this shortcut. This is a great shortcut to use when making individual frames of an animation by hand. Each frame ends up being a composite of the individual layers. After you have the individual layers set up the way you want them for a particular animation frame, create a new empty layer and use this shortcut. Modify the individual layers for the next frame and repeat the process.

Merge a Copy of the Target Layer into the Layer Below

Both: (Option)-Layer→Merge Down; [Alt]+Layer→Merge Down

Mac: Cmd-Option-E

Win: Ctrl+Alt+E

This command merges a copy of the target layer with the layer below it, as long as the layer below the target layer is visible.

Transparency Shortcuts

Toggle Preserve Transparency On and Off for the Target Layer

Both: / (forward slash)

Load Layer Transparency as a Selection

Mac: Cmd-Click on layer

Win: Ctrl+Click on layer

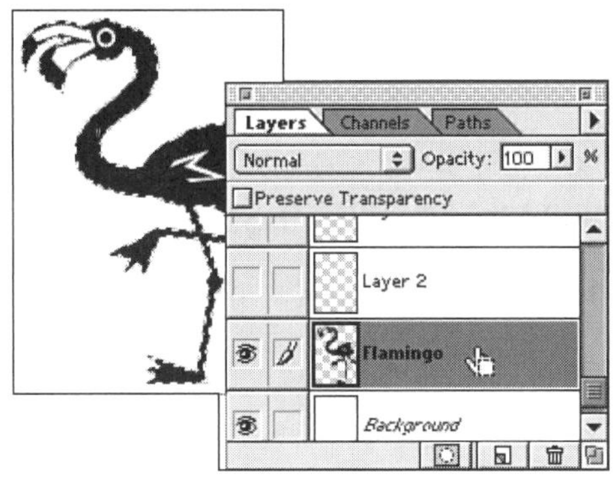

Add Layer Transparency to a Selection

Mac: Cmd-Shift-Click on layer

Win: Ctrl+Shift+Click on layer

Subtract Layer Transparency from a Selection

Mac: Cmd-Option-Click on layer

Win: Ctrl+Alt+Click on layer

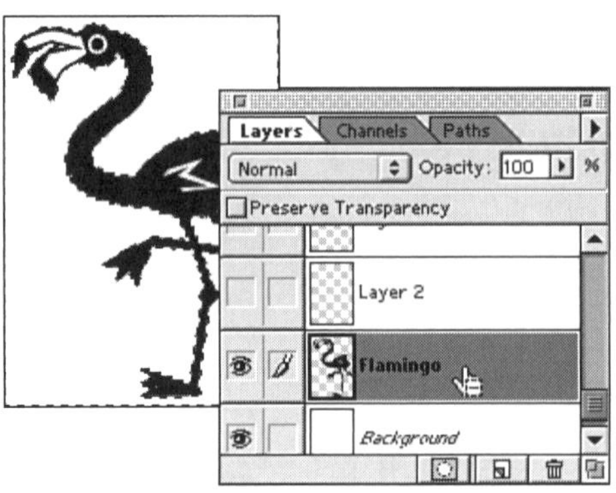

Intersect Layer Transparency with a Selection

Mac: Cmd-Option-Shift-Click on layer

Win: Ctrl+Alt+Shift+Click on layer

Layer Mask Commands

Create Layer Mask with Reveal All/Reveal Selection

Mouse: Click on Layer Mask button

Create Layer Mask with Hide All/Hide Selection

Mac: Option-Click on Layer Mask button

Win: Alt+Click on Layer Mask button

Toggle Layer Mask On/Off

Mouse: Shift+Click on layer mask thumbnail

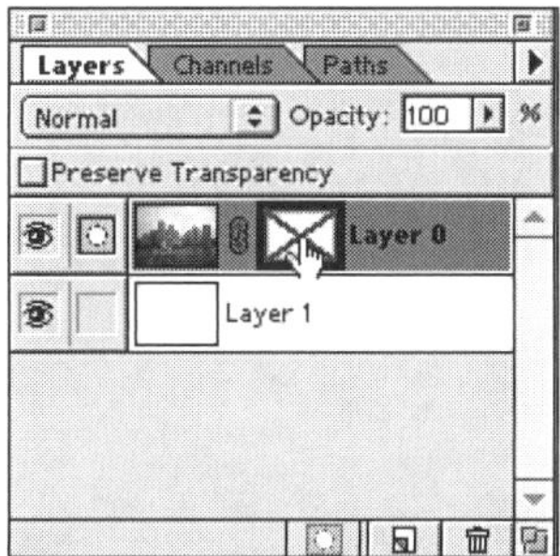

Toggle Between Layer Mask and Composite View

Mac: Option-Click on layer mask thumbnail

Win: Alt+Click on layer mask thumbnail

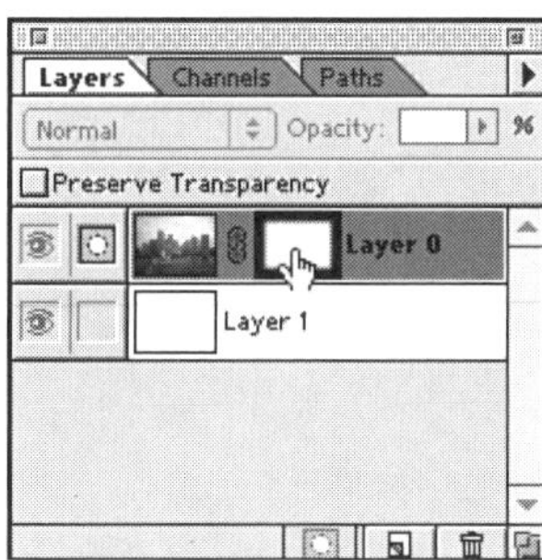

Toggle Rubylith (Mask Overlay) Mode for Layer Mask On/Off

Mac: Option-Shift-Click on layer mask thumbnail

Win: Alt+Shift+Click on layer mask thumbnail

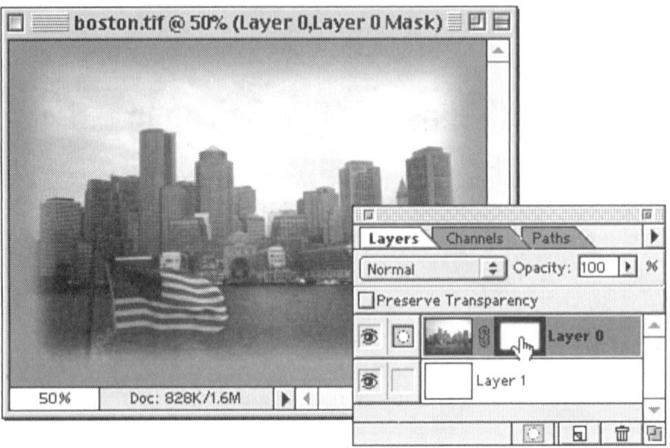

Link/Unlink a Layer Mask with Its Layer

Mouse: Click in the Link Layer Mask icon area

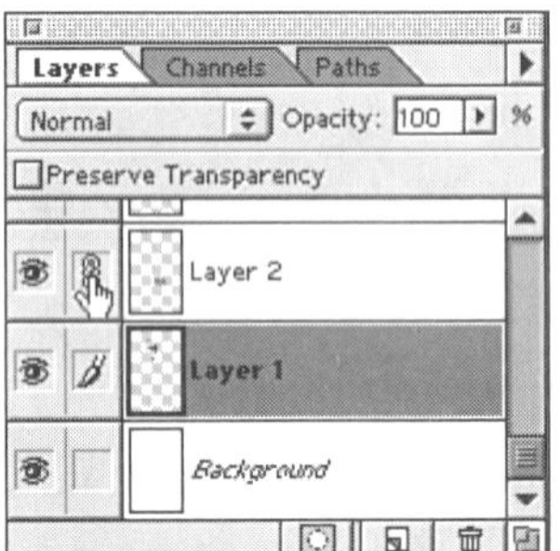

Open the Layer Mask Options Dialog Box

Mouse: Double-click on the Layer Mask icon

Type

Type Commands

Type Tool

Both: T

Cycle Through Type Tools

Both: Shift+T

Toggle to the Eyedropper Tool

Mac: Option

Win: Alt

This shortcut allows you to choose a new foreground color (and the color for the text you are about to create) before entering the Type dialog box and without having to switch tools first. This shortcut works with the Vertical Type tool as well.

Type Editing Commands

Move Cursor One Character Right

Both: Right Arrow

Move Cursor One Character Left

Both: Left Arrow

Move Cursor One Line Up

Both: Up Arrow

Move Cursor One Line Down

Both: Down Arrow

Move Cursor One Word Right

Mac: Cmd-Right Arrow

Win: Ctrl+Right Arrow

Move Cursor One Word Left

Mac: Cmd-Left Arrow

Win: Ctrl+Left Arrow

Type Selection Commands

Select a Word

Both: Double-click on word

Select One Character to the Right

Both: Shift+Right Arrow

Select One Character to the Left

Both: Shift+Left Arrow

Select One Word to the Right

Mac: Cmd-Shift-Right Arrow

Win: Ctrl+Shift+Right Arrow

Select One Word to the Left

Mac: Cmd-Shift-Left Arrow

Win: Ctrl+Shift+Left Arrow

Select One Line Up

Both: Shift+Up Arrow

Select One Line Down

Both: Shift+Down Arrow

Select All

Mac: Cmd-A

Win: Ctrl+A

Select Characters from the Current Insertion Point

Both: Shift+Click

Type Formatting Commands

Increase Text Point Size by 2 Points

Mac: Cmd-Shift->

Win: Ctrl+Shift+>

Decrease Text Point Size by 2 Points

Mac: Cmd-Shift-<

Win: Ctrl+Shift+<

Increase Text Point Size by 10 Points

Mac: Cmd-Option-Shift->

Win: Ctrl+Alt+Shift+>

Decrease Text Point Size by 10 Points

Mac: Cmd-Option-Shift-<

Win: Ctrl+Alt+Shift+<

Increase Leading by 2 Points

Mac: Option-Down Arrow

Win: Alt+Down Arrow

Decrease Leading by 2 Points

Mac: Option-Up Arrow

Win: Alt+Up Arrow

Increase Leading by 10 Points

Mac: Cmd-Option-Down Arrow

Win: Ctrl+Alt+Down Arrow

Decrease Leading by 10 Points

Mac: Cmd-Option-Up Arrow

Win: Ctrl+Alt+Up Arrow

Increase Kerning/Tracking by 2/100 Em Space

Mac: Option-Right Arrow

Win: Alt+Right Arrow

Decrease Kerning/Tracking by 2/100 Em Space

Mac: Option-Left Arrow

Win: Alt+Left Arrow

Increase Kerning/Tracking by 10/100 Em Space

Mac: Cmd-Option-Right Arrow

Win: Ctrl+Alt+Right Arrow

Decrease Kerning/Tracking by 10/100 Em Space

Mac: Cmd-Option-Left Arrow

Win: Ctrl+Alt+Left Arrow

Increase Baseline Shift by 2 Points

Mac: Option-Shift-Up Arrow

Win: Alt+Shift+Up Arrow

Decrease Baseline Shift by 2 Points

Mac: Option-Shift-Down Arrow

Win: Alt+Shift+Down Arrow

Increase Baseline Shift by 10 Points

Mac: Cmd-Option-Shift-Up Arrow

Win: Ctrl+Alt+Shift+Up Arrow

Decrease Baseline Shift by 10 Points

Mac: Cmd-Option-Shift-Down Arrow

Win: Ctrl+Alt+Shift+Down Arrow

Selections

Select Menu Commands

Move Selection Marquee 1 Pixel

Both: Arrow keys

Mouse: With a selection tool active, place cursor inside the selection, then press and drag

As long as a selection tool is active (Marquee, Lasso, Magic Wand), the arrow keys move just the selection marquee—not any pixels—one pixel in the direction of the arrow key you choose.

Move Selection Marquee 10 Pixels

Both: Shift+Arrow keys

Mouse: With a selection tool active, place cursor inside the selection, then press and drag

As long as a selection tool is active (Marquee, Lasso, Magic Wand), holding down the Shift key and then using the arrow keys moves a selection marquee 10 pixels in the direction of the arrow key you choose.

Move Selected Pixels 1 Pixel

Menu: Edit→Transform→Numeric

Both: Arrow keys

Mouse: With the Move tool active, press and drag

As long as the Move tool is active, the arrow keys move selected pixels one pixel in the direction of the arrow key you choose. If any other tool is active, hold down the (Cmd) [Ctrl] key, and then use the arrow keys.

Move Selected Pixels 10 Pixels

Menu: Edit→Transform→Numeric

Both: Shift+Arrow keys

Mouse: With the Move tool active, press and drag

As long as the Move tool is active, holding down the Shift key and then pressing the arrow keys moves selected pixels 10 pixels in the direction of the arrow key you choose. If any other tool is active, hold down the (Cmd-Shift) [Ctrl+Shift] keys, and then use the arrow keys.

Select All

Menu: Select→All

Mac: Cmd-A

Win: Ctrl+A

Deselect

Menu: Select→Deselect

Mac: Cmd-D

Win: Ctrl+D

Reselect

Menu: Select→Reselect

Mac: Cmd-Shift-D

Win: Ctrl+Shift+D

Inverse

Menu: Select→Inverse

Mac: Cmd-Shift-I

Win: Ctrl+Shift+I

Feather

Menu: Select→Feather

Mac: Cmd-Option-D

Win: Ctrl+Option+D

Load Layer Transparency as a Selection

Mac: Cmd-Click on layer

Win: Ctrl+Click on layer

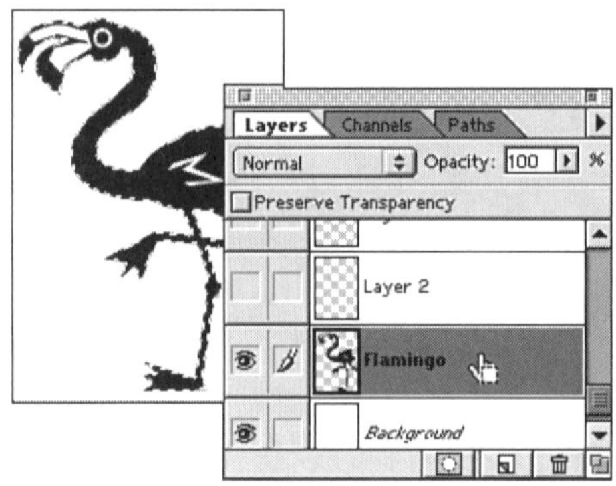

Add Layer Transparency to a Selection

Mac: Cmd-Shift-Click on layer

Win: Ctrl+Shift+Click on layer

Subtract Layer Transparency from a Selection

Mac: Cmd-Option-Click on layer

Win: Ctrl+Alt+Click on layer

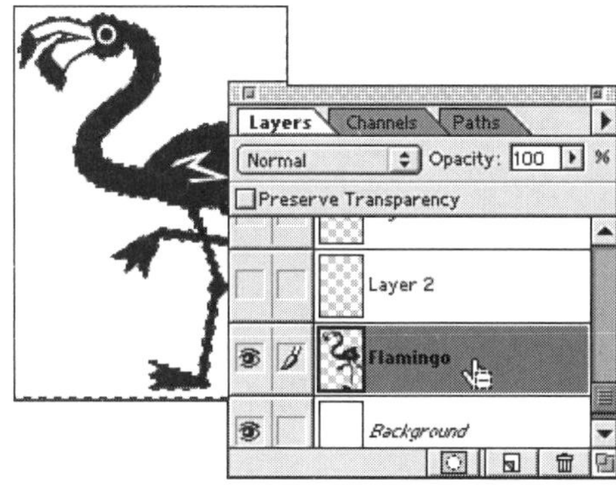

Intersect Layer Transparency with a Selection

Mac: Cmd-Option-Shift-Click on layer

Win: Ctrl+Alt+Shift+Click on layer

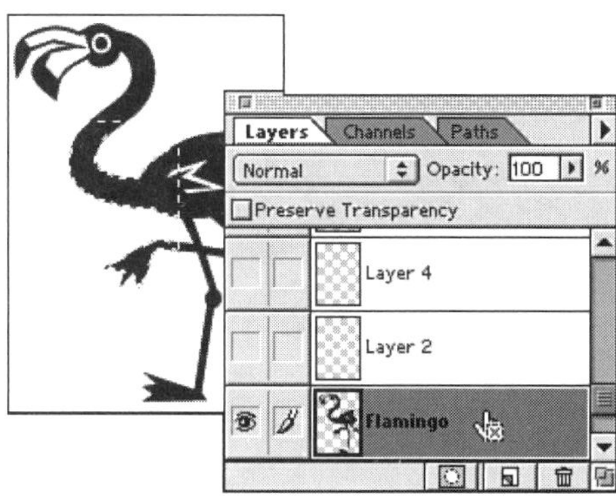

Selection Tool Shortcuts

Add to a Selection

Mouse: Shift+Drag

This shortcut is the same when using any of the selection tools: Rectangular Marquee, Elliptical Marquee, or any of the Lasso tools.

Subtract from a Selection

Mac: Option-Drag

Win: Alt+Drag

This shortcut is the same when using any of the selection tools: Rectangular Marquee, Elliptical Marquee, or any of the Lasso tools.

Intersect with a Selection

Mac: Option-Shift-Drag

Win: Alt+Shift+Drag

This shortcut is the same when using any of the selection tools: Rectangular Marquee, Elliptical Marquee, or any of the Lasso tools.

Constrain to a Square Selection

Mouse: Shift+Drag

This shortcut only works if you are starting a new selection. If a selection already exists, you add to the selection instead.

Constrain to a Circle Selection

Mouse: Shift+Drag

This shortcut only works if you are starting a new selection. If a selection already exists, you add to the selection instead.

Draw from the Center While Creating Selections

Mac: Option-Drag

Win: Alt+Drag

Normally, when creating a selection, the selection anchors itself from wherever you click, creating the selection outward from that position in a diagonal direction. With this shortcut, wherever you click becomes the center of the selection as you create it. Also, remember that this shortcut only works if you are starting a new selection. If a selection already exists, you subtract from the selection instead.

Constrain and Draw from the Center While Creating Selections

Mac: Option-Shift-Drag

Win: Alt+Shift+Drag

Normally, when creating a selection, the selection anchors itself from wherever you click, creating the selection outward from that position in a diagonal direction. With this shortcut, wherever you click becomes the center of the selection as you create it. Also, remember that this shortcut only works if you are starting a new selection. If a selection already exists, you are left with the intersection of the selections instead.

Constrain a Selection as You Move It

Mouse: Shift+Drag

Make sure the cursor is within the selection area and that you press the mouse button down before you hold down the Shift key. If you hold down the Shift key first, you will add to the selection when you start dragging. If the cursor is outside the selected area, you will start a new selection instead of moving the existing one.

Reposition a Selection as You Create It

Both: Spacebar

This is one of my favorite shortcuts. Sometimes you are trying to select a specific shape in an image and halfway through dragging out the selection, you realize you didn't start in the right position. Rather than starting over, just hold down the Spacebar. This allows you to drag the marquee to a different position. When you are ready to continue with the selection, just let go of the Spacebar. Remember to keep the mouse button down until you are finished making the selection.

Duplicate a Selection

Mac: Option-Drag

Win: Alt+Drag

Draw Using the Polygonal Lasso Tool

Mac: Option-Click/Drag

Win: Alt+Click/Drag

This shortcut allows you to temporarily switch to the Polygonal Lasso tool while using the regular Lasso tool.

Draw Using the Lasso Tool

Mac: Option-Click/Drag

Win: Alt+Click/Drag

This shortcut allows you to temporarily switch to the Lasso tool while using the Polygonal Lasso tool.

Magic Wand Shortcuts

Add to a Selection

Mouse: Shift+Click

Subtract from a Selection

Mac: Option-Click

Win: Alt+Click

Intersect with a Selection

Mac: Option-Shift-Click

Win: Alt+Shift+Click

Type Selection Shortcuts

Select a Word

Mouse: Double-click on word

VERSION 5.0

Select One Character to the Right

Both: Shift+Right Arrow

VERSION 5.0

Select One Character to the Left

Both: Shift+Left Arrow

VERSION 5.0

Select One Word to the Right

Mac: Cmd-Shift-Right Arrow

Win: Ctrl+Shift+Right Arrow

VERSION 5.0

Select One Word to the Left

Mac: Cmd-Shift-Left Arrow

Win: Ctrl+Shift+Left Arrow

VERSION 5.0

Select One Line Up

Both: Shift+Up Arrow

VERSION 5.0

Select One Line Down

Both: Shift+Down Arrow

VERSION 5.0

Select All

VERSION 5.0

Mac: Cmd-A

Win: Ctrl+A

Select Characters from the Current Insertion Point

VERSION 5.0

Both: Shift+Click

The **Filters** Menu

Filter Commands

Repeat the Last Filter Used

Menu: Filter→Name of the filter

Mac: Cmd-F

Win: Ctrl+F

This shortcut just applies the last filter you used again; it does not reopen the dialog box of the filter you used last so that you can change the settings before applying again. As you might guess, there is a separate shortcut for that as well.

Reopen the Last Filter Used with Same Settings

Mac: Cmd-Option-F

Win: Ctrl+Alt+F

Lighting Effects

Duplicate Light in Lighting Effects Preview

Mac: Option-Drag light

Win: Alt+Drag light

Delete Light in Lighting Effects Preview

Both: Delete

Adjust Light Footprint Without Changing the Angle

Both: Shift+Drag handle

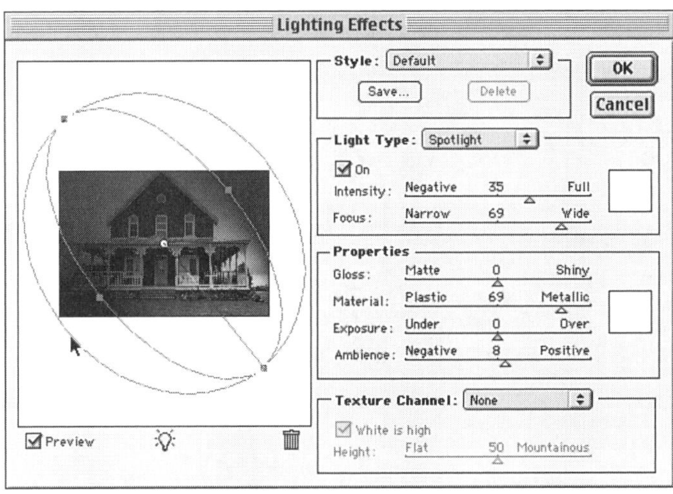

Adjust Light Angle Without Changing the Footprint

Mac: Cmd-Drag handle

Win: Ctrl+Drag handle

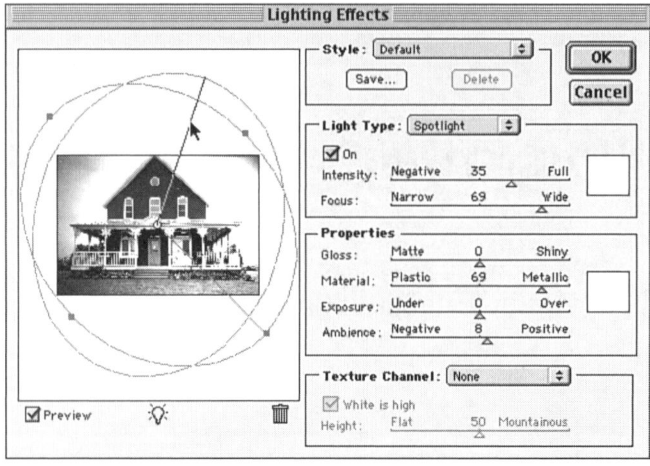

The **View** Menu

View Menu Commands

Toggle Between Document Preview Tabs

Menu: View→Show Original/Optimized/2-Up/4-Up

Mac: Cmd-Y

Win: Ctrl+Y

This shortcut toggles you between the Original, Optimized, 2-Up, and 4-Up tabs in the ImageReady document window.

Preview Browser Dither

Menu: View→Preview→Browser Dither

Mac: Cmd-Shift-Y

Win: Ctrl+Shift+Y

Toggle Through Gamma Previews in the Selected Image Pane

Menu: View→Preview→Preview choice

Mac: Cmd-Option-Y

Win: Ctrl+Alt+Y

Hide Edges

Menu: View→Hide Edges

Mac: Cmd-H

Win: Ctrl+H

Toggle Show/Hide Rulers

Menu: View→Show/Hide Rulers

Mac: Cmd-R

Win: Ctrl+R

Toggle Show/Hide Guides

Menu: View→Show/Hide Guides

Mac: Cmd-; (semicolon)

Win: Ctrl+; (semicolon)

Toggle Snap to Guides

Menu: View→Snap to Guides

Mac: Cmd-Shift-; (semicolon)

Win: Ctrl+Shift+; (semicolon)

Toggle Lock/Unlock Guides

Menu: View→Lock Guides

Mac: Cmd-Option-; (semicolon)

Win: Ctrl+Alt+; (semicolon)

Toggle Show/Hide Grid

Menu: View→Show Grid

Mac: Cmd-' (apostrophe)

Win: Ctrl+' (apostrophe)

Toggle Snap to Grid

Menu: View→Snap to Grid

Mac: Cmd-Shift-' (apostrophe)

Win: Ctrl+Shift+' (apostrophe)

Snap Guide to Ruler

Both: Shift+Drag guide

Toggle Guide Orientation

Mac: Option-Drag guide

Win: Alt+Drag guide

The **Window** Menu

Window Menu Commands

Close All Documents

Menu: Window→Close All

Mac: Cmd-Shift-W

Win: Ctrl+Shift+W

Show or Hide the Optimize Palette

Menu: Window→Show/Hide Optimize

Both: F10

Show or Hide the Info Palette

Menu: Window→Show/Hide Info

Both: F8

Open the Options Palette

Menu: Window→Show/Hide Options

Both: Enter or Return

Mouse: Double-click on a tool

Show or Hide the Color Palette

Menu: Window→Show/Hide Color

Both: F6

Show or Hide the Swatches Palette

Menu: Window→Show/Hide Swatches

Both: F6

F6 shows or hides the Color palette. Also use it to show or hide the Swatches palette. To show Swatches if the Color palette is not open, press F6, and then click on the Swatches tab. To hide both the Swatches and the Color palettes, press the F6 key until they both disappear.

Show or Hide the Brushes Palette

Menu: Window→Show/Hide Brushes

Both: F5

Show or Hide the Layers Palette

Menu: Window→Show/Hide Layers

Both: F7

Show or Hide the Animation Palette

Menu: Window→Show/Hide Animation

Both: F11

Show or Hide the Slice Palette

Menu: Window→Show/Hide Slice

Both: F11

F11 shows or hides the Animation palette. Also use it to show or hide the Slice palette. To show Slice if the Animation palette is not open, press F11, and then click on the Slice tab. To hide both the Slice and the Animation palettes, press the F11 key until they both disappear.

Show or Hide the Rollover Palette

Menu: Window→Show/Hide Rollover

Both: F11

F11 shows or hides the Animation palette. Also use it to show or hide the Rollover palette. To show Rollover if the Animation palette is not open, press F11, and then click on the Rollover tab. To hide both the Rollover and the Animation palettes, press the F11 key until they both disappear.

PART THREE

Extras

Actions

Photoshop Power Shortcuts would be incomplete if I didn't mention the capability to create your own custom shortcuts using Actions. Actions first arrived in Photoshop 4. Photoshop 5 vastly improved what Actions can do by increasing the amount of things that can be recorded. Just about everything can be recorded with a few notable exceptions. My favorite improvement—changing a layer's blend mode and opacity—can now be recorded. You can use Actions to assign an F key (Function key) to any menu command that doesn't already have one, and you can use Actions to record many steps and then play those steps back on a batch of files.

In addition to the actual keyboard shortcuts for the Actions palette, here are 10 general tips to help you when working with Actions.

Top Ten Action Tips

1. When you record an Action, Photoshop records what happened—not what you did. For instance, when you record the Select All command, you see "Set Selection" listed in the Action commands list. In other words, you need to learn to speak "Actionese." It is often helpful to click the triangle next to each command in the Action list to see the contents of an Action for it to make sense. In the previous Set Selection example, if you turn down the arrow, you see that it says, "To: All."
2. Actions are literal! That means if you select a layer by clicking its layer name in the Layers palette, the name of the layer is recorded as well. This can cause problems on playback. For instance, if you record clicking a layer named "bob" and the file you play the Action back in does not have a layer in it named "bob," your Action will not work like you wanted it to. Most of the time it is better to record layers by their position and not their name, so use the keyboard shortcuts to select and move layers. (See pages 111–117 if you need a reminder.)
3. To save your Actions so that they can be shared across platforms, make sure they are named with the .atn file extension.
4. If your Actions require a specific start state to work correctly, such as the image must be in the RGB mode, be sure to document this some way. The easiest way to do this is to include a comment in the Action's name. For more complex situations, insert a Stop command and enter a comment. When the Action is played, a dialog box appears with the text you entered.

5. You can record image adjustments that rely on saved settings, such as Curves or Levels saved settings. In those instances, the Action records the pathname to the file you saved or loaded while you were recording. However, if you want to distribute the Action without those accompanying saved files, you have to trick Photoshop into embedding the saved settings.

   To do this—say, for the example a Curves setting loaded from disk—double-click the Curves command in the Action. Add a point to the curve, and then click OK. Repeat this process, except delete the curve point you added previously; the Action now contains a complete description of the loaded curve. Similar workarounds work for other adjustments.

6. To rerecord an Action step, just double-click it.
7. If you just want to have a particular dialog box appear (such as Gaussian Blur) so that you can enter your own values, don't record opening the dialog box from its menu. Instead, use Insert Menu Command. This opens a dialog box for you to type the menu command you want. You can also just choose the menu command you want from the actual menu, and it inserts the command for you.
8. To play a single step of an Action, hold down the (Cmd) [Ctrl] key and double-click it.
9. To make the Batch command work faster, change the Cache Levels setting to 1 in the Image Cache Preferences, and turn off the History palette's automatic snapshot feature. (Note: Special thanks to Deke McClelland for that tip.)
10. The Move tool looks like it doesn't get recorded because you don't see any Action listed in the command list after you've moved something. To make the Move command appear in the command list, you have to do something else first. This is because Photoshop is waiting to see if you are going to move the layer or selection somewhere else before moving on to your next step.

Action Commands

Select Multiple Commands in the Actions List

Both: Shift+Click

Play an Action

Menu: Actions→Play

Mac: Cmd-Double-click on action

Win: Ctrl+Double-click on action

Both: Click the Play button

Play Just a Single Step of an Action

Mac: Cmd-Double-click on step

Win: Ctrl+Double-click on step

Both: (Cmd-Click) the Play button; [Ctrl+Click] the Play button

Toggle an Action Step On/Off

Both: Click on Checkmark icon area

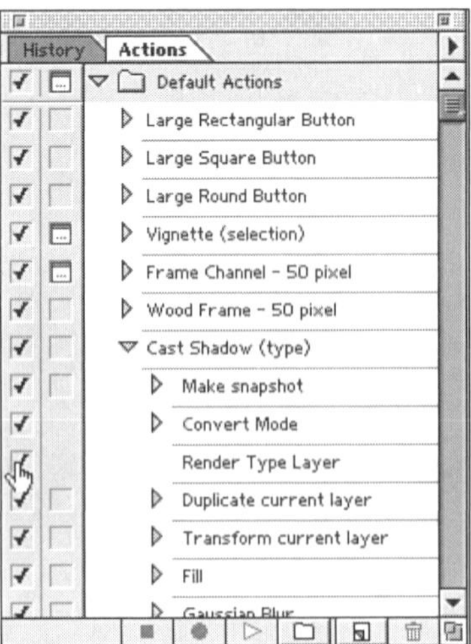

Toggle All Other Action Steps On/Off for This Action

Mac: Option-Click the Checkmark icon area

Win: Alt+Click the Checkmark icon area

Toggle Dialogs for an Action Step On/Off

Both: Click the Dialog icon area

Toggle Dialogs for All Steps of an Action On/Off

Both: Click the Dialog icon area next to name of action

Toggle All Commands for a Set of Actions On/Off

Both: Click the Checkmark icon area for set

Toggle All Dialogs for a Set of Actions On/Off

Both: Click the Dialog icon area for set

Edit Action Options

Both: Double-click item

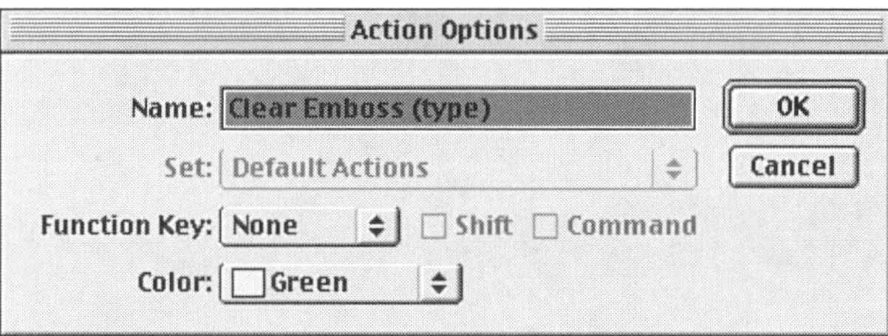

Create New Action

Menu: Action Palette→New Action

Both: Click the New Action button

Create New Action and Skip the Dialog Box

Mac: Option-Click the New Action button

Win: Alt+Click the New Action button

View/Hide All Steps of All Actions in a Set

Mac: Option-Click the triangle next to the set name

Win: Alt+Click the triangle next to the set name

Toggle Dialogs for All Other Steps of an Action On/Off

Mac: Option-Click the Dialog icon area next to step you want to leave on

Win: Alt+Click the Dialog icon area next to step you want to leave on

Easter Eggs

Easter Eggs

Version 4 Secret Splash Screen

VERSION 4.0

Mac: Hold down Cmd and choose Apple Menu→About Photoshop

Win: Hold down Ctrl and choose Help→About Photoshop

Impress your friends with this piece of trivia: The code name for Photoshop 4 while it was under development was Big Electric Cat. This secret splash screen was created by Joseph Kelter.

Adobe
Licensed to: Kate Binder
Prospect Hill
PSW251B3124839-177
Adobe® Photoshop® 4.0 PowerPC™
Thomas Knoll, Mark Hamburg, Seetha Narayanan, Sean Parent, Greg Gilley, Laura Hoffman,
Jason Bartell, Scott Byer, Allen Chan, Jeff Chien, Tom Costa, David DiGiacomo, Andrei Herasimchuk,
Charles McBrian, Marc Pawliger, Anapathur Ramesh, Akiko Sonoda, Robert Swirsky-Warner,
Doug Ahmann, Doug Olson, Paul Holland, Andrew Coven, John Leddy, Kevin Connor, Russell Brown
Protected by U.S. Patents 5,146,346, 5,546,528, and 4,837,613. Patents pending.
©1989-1996 Adobe Systems, Incorporated. All rights reserved.
Adobe, the Adobe logo and Photoshop are trademarks of Adobe Systems, Inc.
PANTONE® and PANTONE CALIBRATED™ are trademarks of Pantone, Inc.
MacApp® ©1985-1993 Apple Computer, Inc.

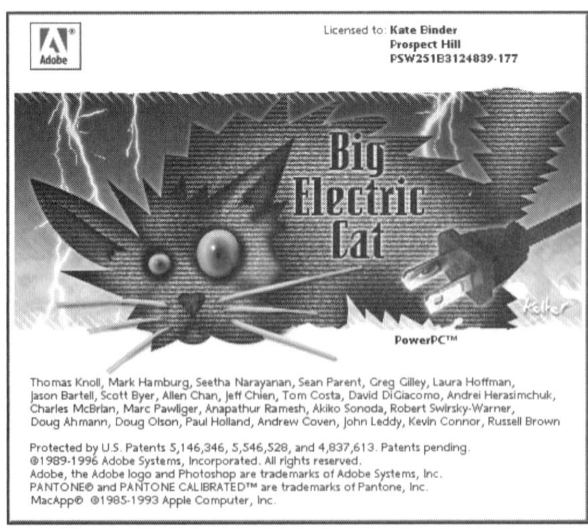
Adobe
Licensed to: Kate Binder
Prospect Hill
PSW251B3124839-177
Big
Electric
Cat
Kelter
PowerPC™
Thomas Knoll, Mark Hamburg, Seetha Narayanan, Sean Parent, Greg Gilley, Laura Hoffman,
Jason Bartell, Scott Byer, Allen Chan, Jeff Chien, Tom Costa, David DiGiacomo, Andrei Herasimchuk,
Charles McBrian, Marc Pawliger, Anapathur Ramesh, Akiko Sonoda, Robert Swirsky-Warner,
Doug Ahmann, Doug Olson, Paul Holland, Andrew Coven, John Leddy, Kevin Connor, Russell Brown
Protected by U.S. Patents 5,146,346, 5,546,528, and 4,837,613. Patents pending.
©1989-1996 Adobe Systems, Incorporated. All rights reserved.
Adobe, the Adobe logo and Photoshop are trademarks of Adobe Systems, Inc.
PANTONE® and PANTONE CALIBRATED™ are trademarks of Pantone, Inc.
MacApp® ©1985-1993 Apple Computer, Inc.

Reveal the Engineer's Secret Comments

VERSION 4.0

You must open the secret splash screen. If you wait a little while, you see the engineering credits start to scroll. To make the credits scroll faster, hold down (Option) [Alt]. After the engineering credits have finished scrolling, (Option-Click)[Alt+Click] in the whitespace directly under the Adobe logo, and you will see their comments appear, one at a time. There are a lot of them, and some of them are very funny.

Keep watching the engineering credits as well, because at the end of those, you will see that the Photoshop team actually thanks you personally as well, and lets you know that you are one of their favorite customers.

Version 5/5.5 Secret Splash Screen

VERSION 5.0

VERSION 5.5

Mac: Hold down Cmd and choose Apple Menu→About Photoshop

Win: Hold down Ctrl and choose Help→About Photoshop

Impress your friends with this piece of trivia: The code name for Photoshop 5 while it was under development was Strange Cargo. Apparently, there was no code name for Photoshop 5.5, so there isn't a new secret splash screen. This secret splash screen was created by Jeff Schewe, one of the external Alpha Team members for Photoshop 5.

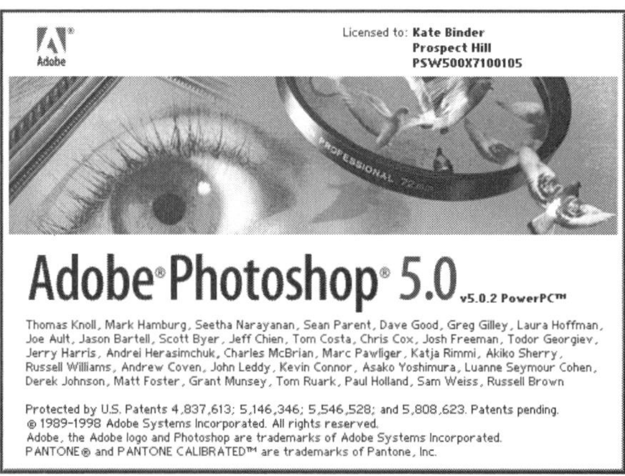

Adobe
Licensed to: Kate Binder
Prospect Hill
PSW500X7100105
PROFESSIONAL
Adobe® Photoshop® 5.0 v5.0.2 PowerPC™
Thomas Knoll, Mark Hamburg, Seetha Narayanan, Sean Parent, Dave Good, Greg Gilley, Laura Hoffman, Joe Ault, Jason Bartell, Scott Byer, Jeff Chien, Tom Costa, Chris Cox, Josh Freeman, Todor Georgiev, Jerry Harris, Andrei Herasimchuk, Charles McBrian, Marc Pawliger, Katja Rimmi, Akiko Sherry, Russell Williams, Andrew Coven, John Leddy, Kevin Connor, Asako Yoshimura, Luanne Seymour Cohen, Derek Johnson, Matt Foster, Grant Munsey, Tom Ruark, Paul Holland, Sam Weiss, Russell Brown
Protected by U.S. Patents 4,837,613; 5,146,346; 5,546,528; and 5,808,623. Patents pending.
© 1989-1998 Adobe Systems Incorporated. All rights reserved.
Adobe, the Adobe logo and Photoshop are trademarks of Adobe Systems Incorporated.
PANTONE® and PANTONE CALIBRATED™ are trademarks of Pantone, Inc.

Adobe
v5.0.2 PowerPC™
Licensed to: Kate Binder
Prospect Hill
PSW500X7100105
STRANGE
SCHEWE
Thomas Knoll, Mark Hamburg, Seetha Narayanan, Sean Parent, Dave Good, Greg Gilley, Laura Hoffman, Joe Ault, Jason Bartell, Scott Byer, Jeff Chien, Tom Costa, Chris Cox, Josh Freeman, Todor Georgiev, Jerry Harris, Andrei Herasimchuk, Charles McBrian, Marc Pawliger, Katja Rimmi, Akiko Sherry, Russell Williams, Andrew Coven, John Leddy, Kevin Connor, Asako Yoshimura, Luanne Seymour Cohen, Derek Johnson, Matt Foster, Grant Munsey, Tom Ruark, Paul Holland, Sam Weiss, Russell Brown
Protected by U.S. Patents 4,837,613; 5,146,346; 5,546,528; and 5,808,623. Patents pending.
© 1989-1998 Adobe Systems Incorporated. All rights reserved.
Adobe, the Adobe logo and Photoshop are trademarks of Adobe Systems Incorporated.
PANTONE® and PANTONE CALIBRATED™ are trademarks of Pantone, Inc.

Reveal the Engineer's Secret Comments

VERSION 5.0 VERSION 5.5

You must open the secret splash screen. If you wait a little while, you see the engineering credits start to scroll. To make the credits scroll faster, hold down (Option) [Alt]. After the engineering credits have finished scrolling, (Cmd-Click)[Ctrl+Click] in the whitespace directly under Jeff Schewe's signature, which is in the lower-left corner of the artwork, and you will see their comments appear, one at a time. There are a lot of them, and some of them are very funny.

Keep watching the engineering credits as well, because at the end of those, you will see a special message to you personally from the Photoshop team.

Reveal Secret Pictures

VERSION 5.0 VERSION 5.5

What happens if you open Photoshop backward…

This easter egg is really buried! First, open the secret splash screen. Then, take a screen shot of the secret splash screen. On the Mac, use Cmd-Shift-3. This creates a Picture 1 file on your hard drive. Open this file in Photoshop. On Windows, press the Print Screen button, create a new file, and paste.

After you have the screen shot open in Photoshop, view it at 100%. Then, view just the Blue channel by pressing (Cmd-3) [Ctrl+3]. Contrary to the rumors, the face in the picture is not Bill Gates—it's Marc Pawlinger, a

Senior Scientist on the Photoshop engineering team. The eye in the sun belongs to Mark Hamburg, another Senior Scientist on the team.

Make the Cat Burp

VERSION 4.0

Mac: Hold down Cmd and click the cat's nose.

Sorry, this is Mac only. You can make the Big Electric Cat burp. First, open the secret splash screen, then hold down the Cmd key and click its nose. I have spoken at countless Photoshop conferences and seminars, and have taught thousands of people over the years. It always seems that THIS is the one secret shortcut that everyone frantically writes down whenever they see it. Go figure, we are easily entertained. Now if I could only remember how to find the flight simulator in Microsoft Excel…

Make the Cat Burp, Again

VERSION 5.0

Both: Type the word "burp" without the quotes

VERSION 5.5

If you look at the top of the box floating in the water in the secret splash screen for Photoshop 5/5.5, you will see that Udo, the Big Electric Cat lives on! Type in his name, Udo, and you will discover that Udo is actually trapped in the box! (The box opens slightly and Udo meows). Type the word "burp" without the quotes and you will hear Udo's updated digital burp.

Make the Cat Meow

VERSION 5.0

Both: Type the word "udo" without the quotes

VERSION 5.5

If you look at the top of the box floating in the water in the secret splash screen for Photoshop 5/5.5, you see that Udo, the Big Electric Cat lives on! Type in his name, Udo, and you will discover that Udo is actually trapped in the box! (The box opens slightly and Udo meows). Type the word "burp" without the quotes and you will hear Udo's updated digital burp.

Find Merlin

Both: Hold down the (Option) key and choose Palette Options from the Layers palette options menu; hold down the [Alt] key and choose Palette Options from the Layers palette options menu.

Reveal the Duck

VERSION 2.0

Mac: (Option+Click) the picture at the top of the toolbar

Win: [Alt+Click] the picture at the top of the toolbar

Both: Hold down the (Option) key and choose Layer Options from the Layers palette options menu; hold down the [Alt] key and choose Layer Options from the Layers palette options menu.

Reveal the Duckerboard

VERSION 2.0

Both: Type "duckerboard" without the quotes

This random shortcut replaces the transparency checkerboard pattern with a duckerboard pattern. To reset it back to the normal checkerboard pattern, just retype "duckerboard."

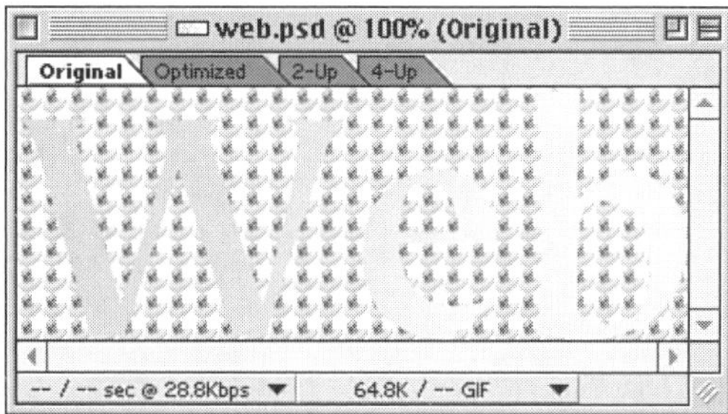

Contextual Menus

Contextual Menus

Don't forget about what perhaps is the single biggest time-saving feature of them all: contextual menus. Contextual menus provide you with literally hundreds of additional shortcuts. Too many people forget to incorporate this feature into their workflow.

I think my favorite contextual menu shortcut is using the Render Layer command from the contextual menu you get when you (Ctrl-Click) [Right-click] on a Type layer. The following pages provide you with screen shots of contextual menus for tools, palettes, and other features. Look them over to see if there is a shortcut you didn't know existed previously, and then take advantage of it.

Photoshop Tool Contextual Menus

Select All
Duplicate Layer...
Delete Layer
Layer Options...
Free Transform
Numeric Transform
Color Range...
Load Selection...
Reselect

Marquee and Lasso tools without selection made.

Deselect
Select Inverse
Feather...
Save Selection...
Make Work Path...
Layer Via Copy
Layer Via Cut
New Layer...
New Adjustment Layer...
Free Transform
Numeric Transform
Transform Selection
Fill...
Stroke...
Last Filter
Fade...

Marquee and Lasso tools with selection made.

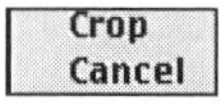

Crop
Cancel

Crop tool with cropping selection made.

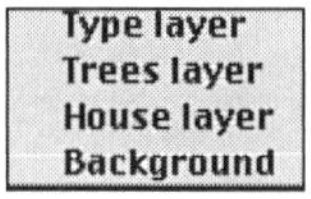

Type layer
Trees layer
House layer
Background

Move tool—lists all the layers immediately below your cursor that have content on them.

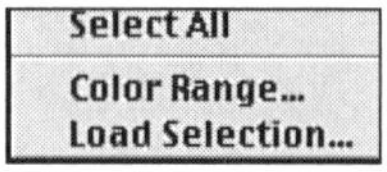

Select All
Color Range...
Load Selection...

Magic Wand tool.

Next Brush
Previous Brush
First Brush
Last Brush
Normal
Dissolve
Behind
Multiply
Screen
Overlay
Soft Light
Hard Light
Color Dodge
Color Burn
Darken
Lighten
Difference
Exclusion
Hue
Saturation
Color
Luminosity

The painting tools—Airbrush, Paintbrush, Rubber Stamp, Pattern Stamp, and Pencil.

New
Snapshot 1
Snapshot 2

Normal
Dissolve
Behind

Multiply
Screen
Overlay
Soft Light
Hard Light

Color Dodge
Color Burn

Darken
Lighten
Difference
Exclusion

History Brush tool—available snapshots are listed in the first section of the contextual menu.

Next Brush
Previous Brush

First Brush
Last Brush

Tight Short
Tight Medium
Tight Long
Loose Medium
Loose Long
Dab
Tight Curl
Tight Curl Long
Loose Curl
Loose Curl Long

Art History Brush tool.

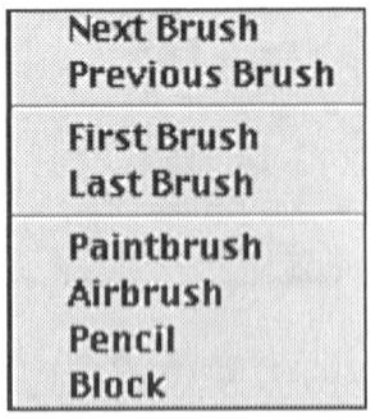

Next Brush
Previous Brush

First Brush
Last Brush

Paintbrush
Airbrush
Pencil
Block

Eraser tool.

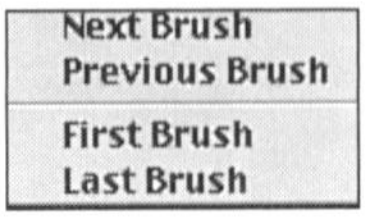

Next Brush
Previous Brush

First Brush
Last Brush

Background Eraser tool.

Normal
Dissolve
Behind
Clear

Multiply
Screen
Overlay
Soft Light
Hard Light

Color Dodge
Color Burn

Darken
Lighten
Difference
Exclusion

Hue
Saturation
Color
Luminosity

Line tool—set the blend mode before drawing.

Next Brush
Previous Brush

First Brush
Last Brush

Normal

Darken
Lighten

Hue
Saturation
Color
Luminosity

Blur, Sharpen, and Smudge tools.

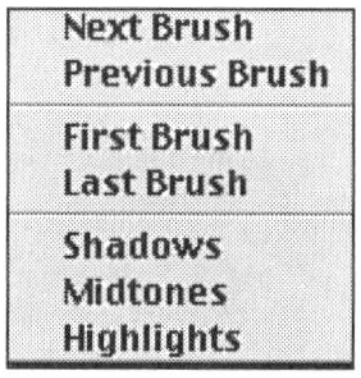

Next Brush
Previous Brush

First Brush
Last Brush

Shadows
Midtones
Highlights

Dodge and Burn tools.

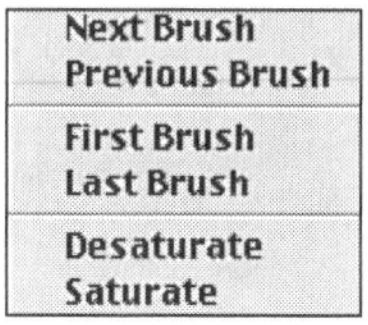

Next Brush
Previous Brush

First Brush
Last Brush

Desaturate
Saturate

Sponge tool.

Delete Path
Turn Off Path
Make Selection...
Fill Path...
Stroke Path...
Clipping Path...
Free Transform Path

Pen tool—if you are on an existing path, the Add Anchor Point option also appears. If you are on a point in an existing path, the Delete Anchor Point option also appears.

Edit Type...
Render Layer
✓ Horizontal
Vertical
Effects...

Type and Vertical Type Mask tools.

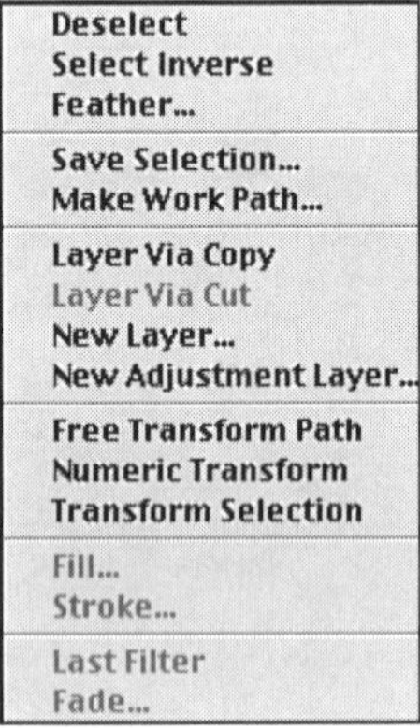

Type Mask and Vertical Type tools.

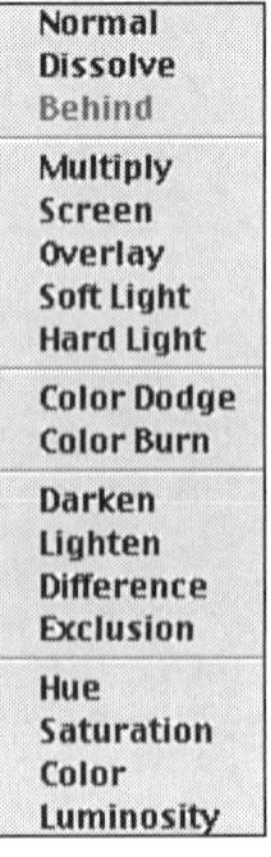

Gradient tool—set the blend mode of the gradient before you create it.

Point Sample
3 by 3 Average
5 by 5 Average
Copy Color as HTML

Eyedropper tool.

Fit on Screen
Actual Pixels
Print Size

Hand tool.

Fit on Screen
Actual Pixels
Print Size
Zoom In
Zoom Out

Zoom tool.

Photoshop Palette Contextual Menus

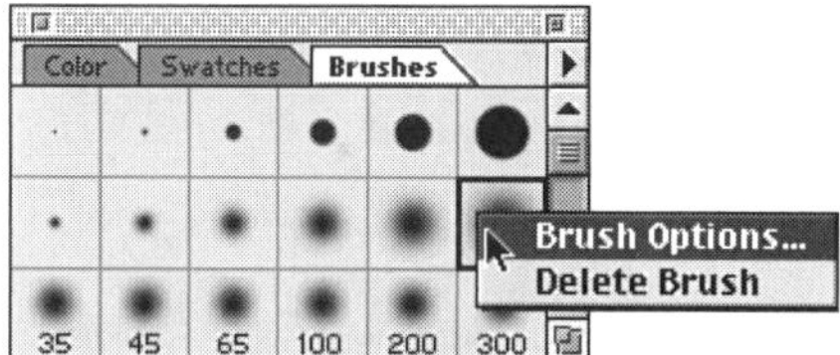

Brushes palette.

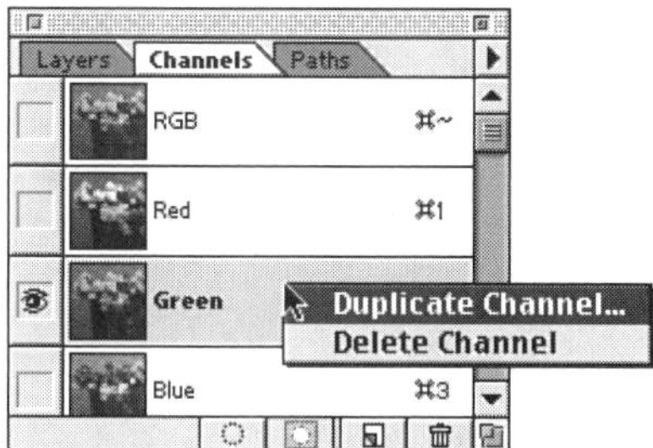

Channels palette.

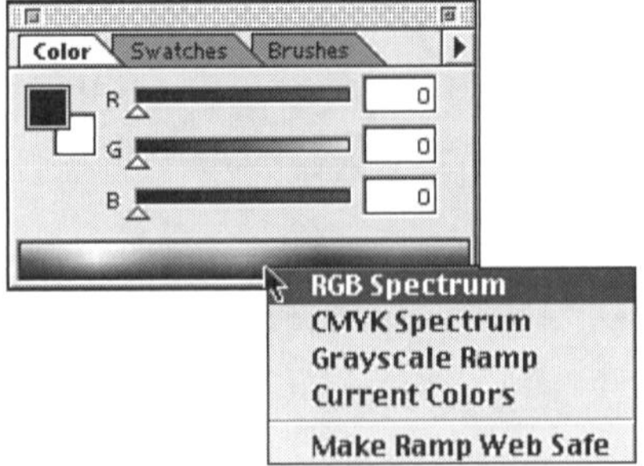

Color palette.

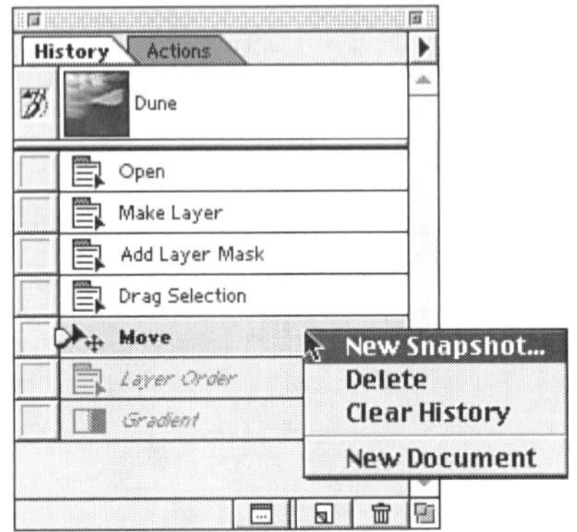

History palette.

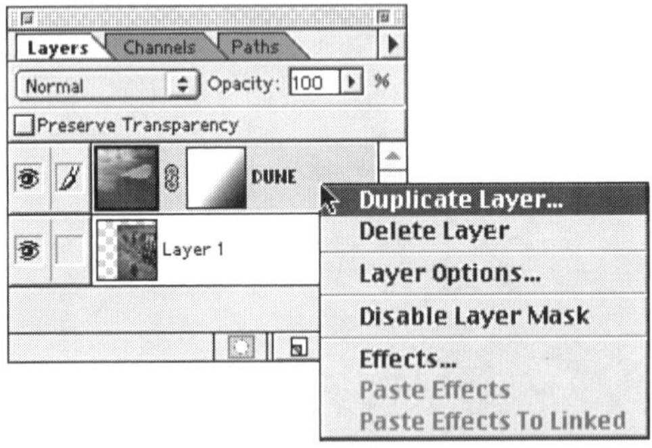

Layers palette.

Layer visibility control.

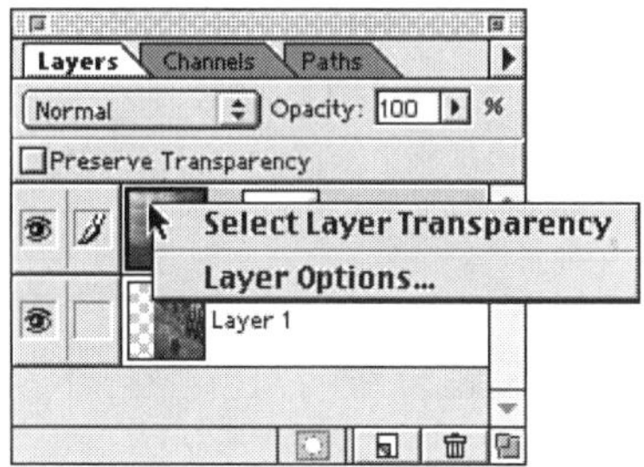

Layer options control.

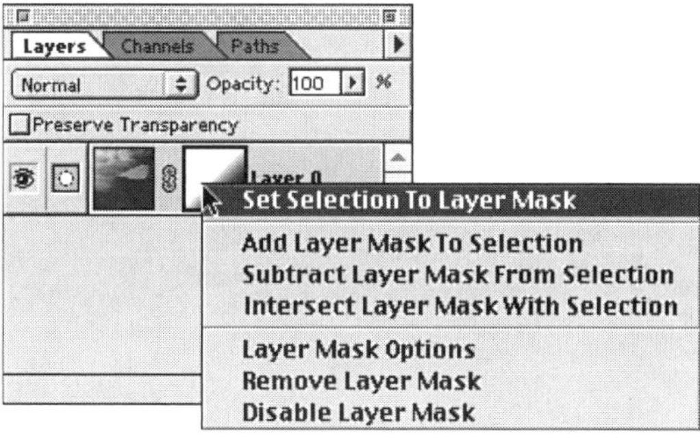

Layer mask control.

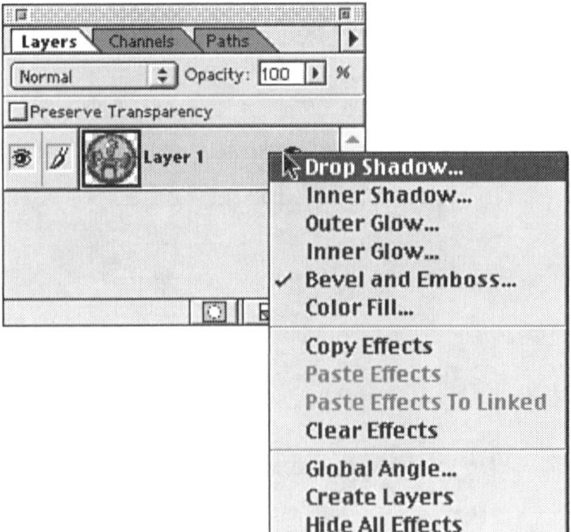

Layer effects control.

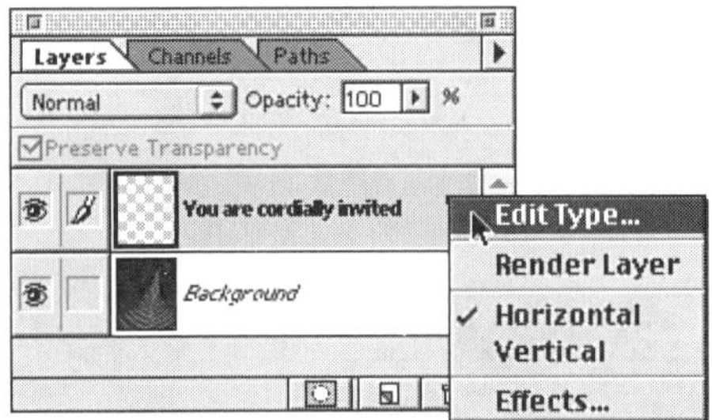

Type Layer control.

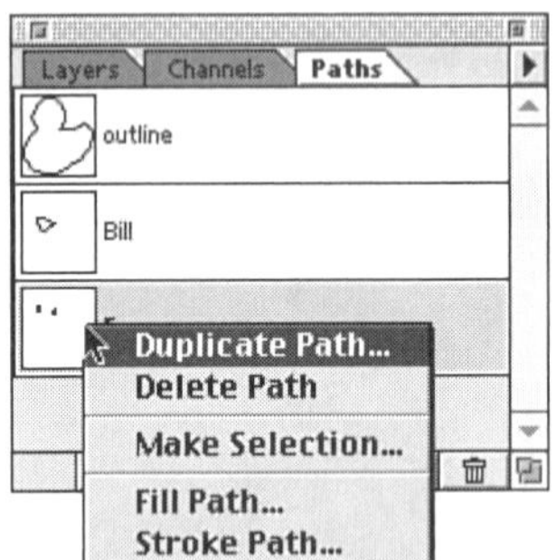

Paths palette.

ImageReady Contextual Menus

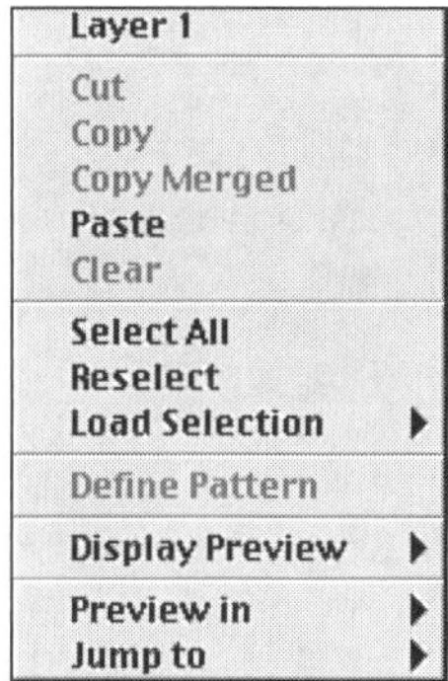

Marquee and Lasso tools without selection made.

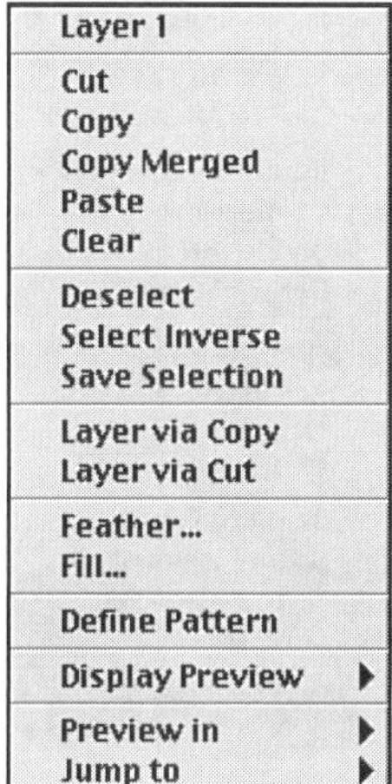

Marquee and Lasso tools with selection made.

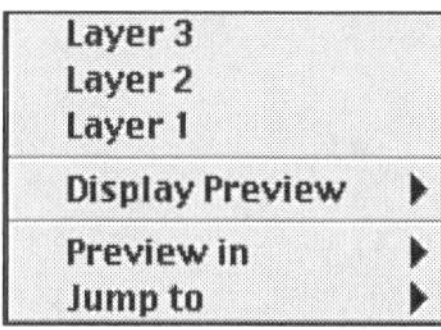

Move tool—lists all the layers immediately below your cursor that have content on them.

Layer 0
Cut
Copy
Copy Merged
Paste
Clear
Deselect
Select Inverse
Save Selection
Layer via Copy
Layer via Cut
Feather...
Fill...
Display Preview ▶
Preview in ▶
Jump to ▶

Magic Wand tool.

Slice and Slice Select tools.

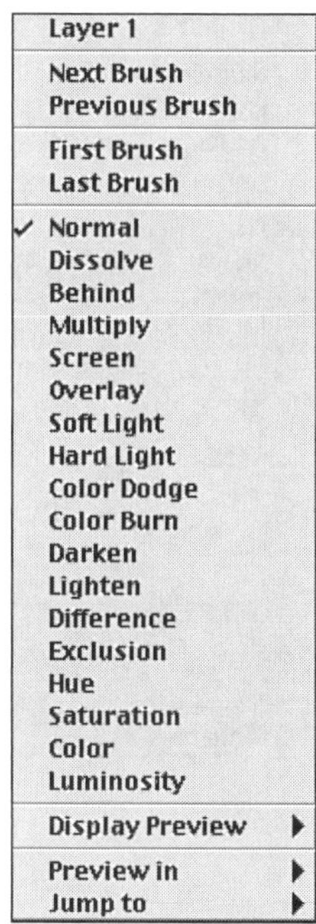

The painting tools—Airbrush, Paintbrush, Rubber Stamp, and Pencil.

Rectangle, Rounded Rectangle, and Ellipse tools.

Eraser tool.

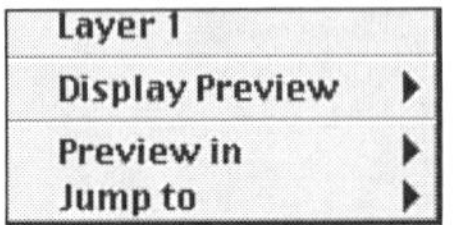

Magic Eraser tool.

Line and Paint Bucket tools—set the blend mode of the tool before using it.

Blur, Sharpen, and Smudge tools.

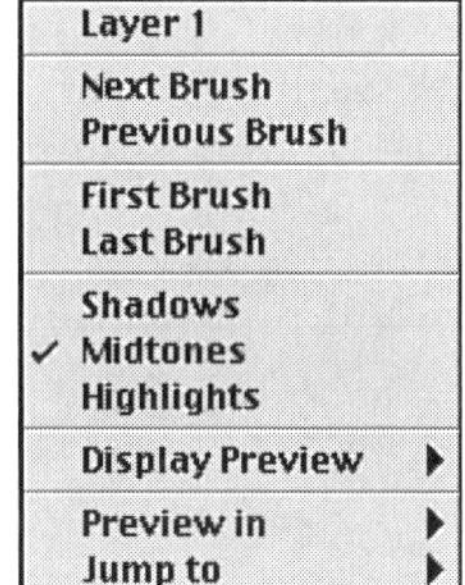

Dodge and Burn tools.

Layer 1
Next Brush
Previous Brush
First Brush
Last Brush
Saturate
✓ Desaturate
Display Preview
Preview in
Jump to

Sponge tool.

Type and Vertical Type tools.

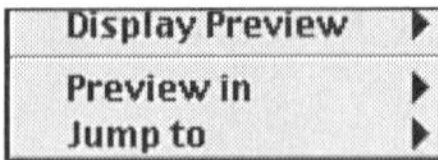

Crop tool.

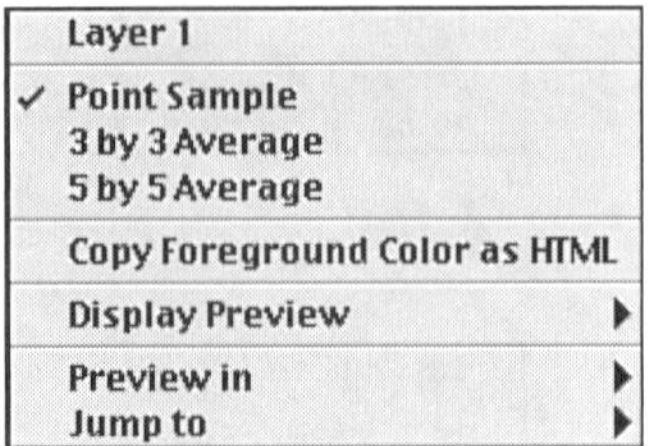

Eyedropper tool.

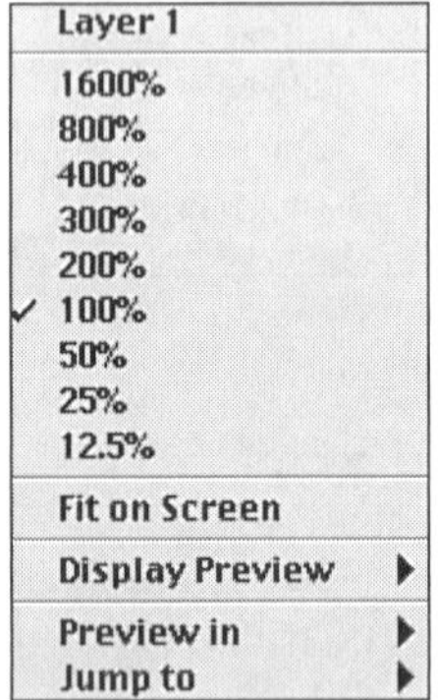

Hand and Zoom tools.

ImageReady Palette Contextual Menus

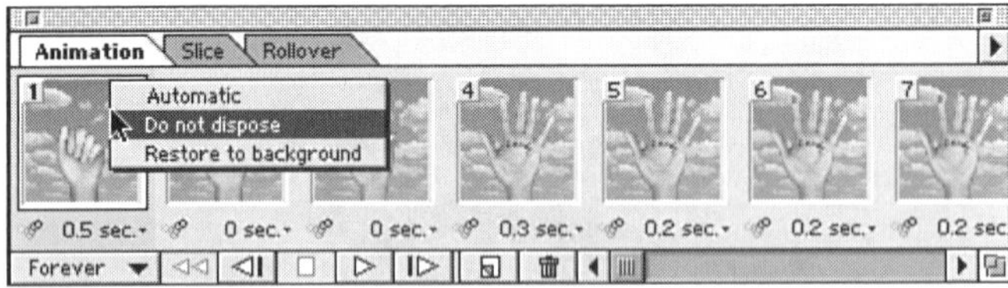

Animation palette.

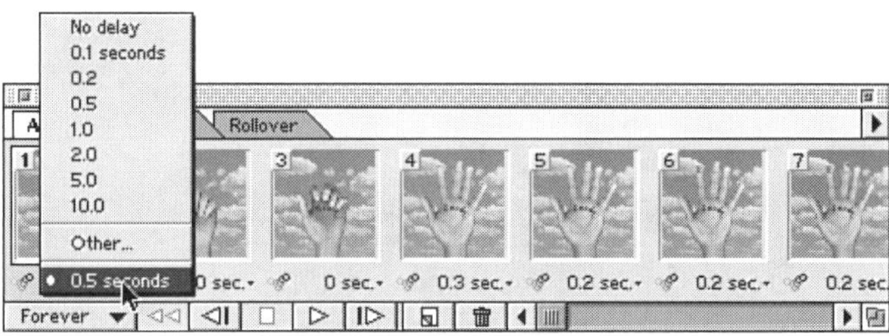

Animation palette.

Slice palette.

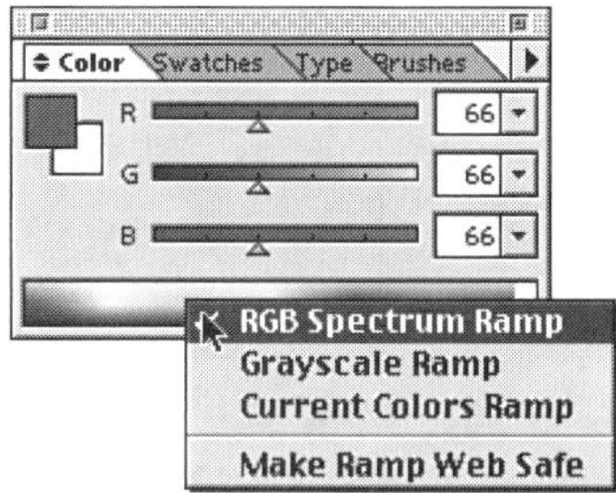

Color palette.

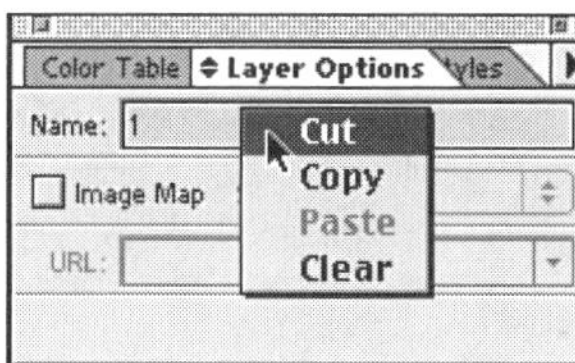

Layer Options palette.

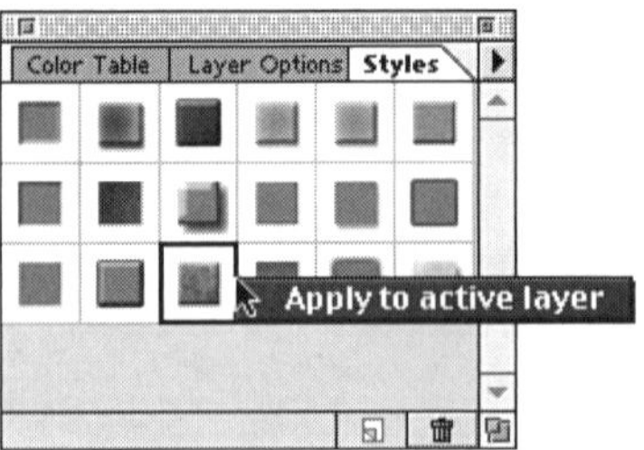

Style palette.

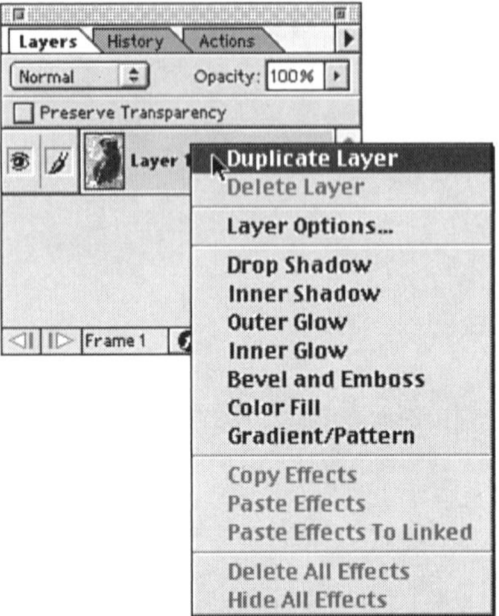

Layers palette (without effects applied).

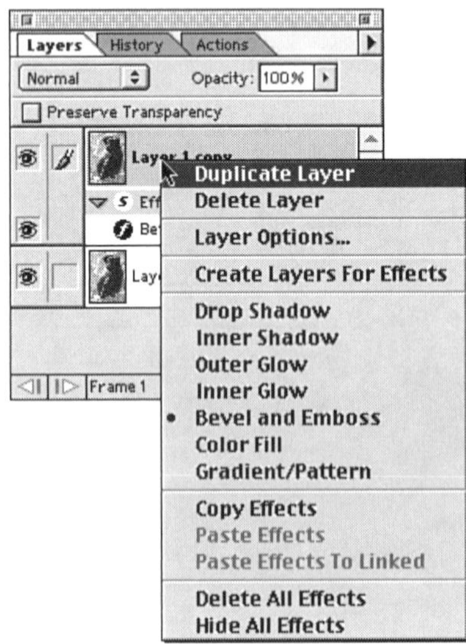

Layers palette (with layer effects applied).

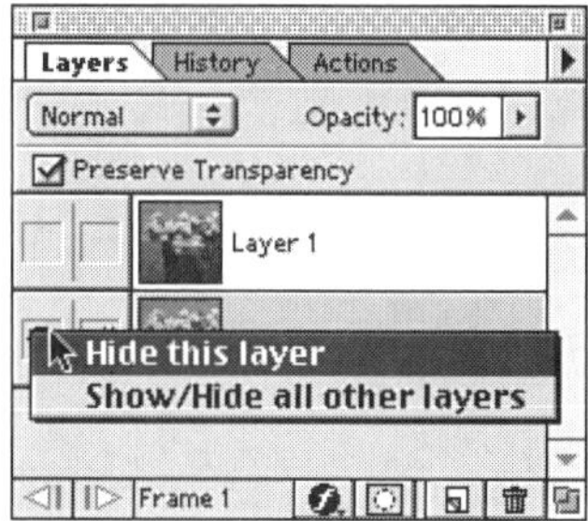

Layer visibility control.

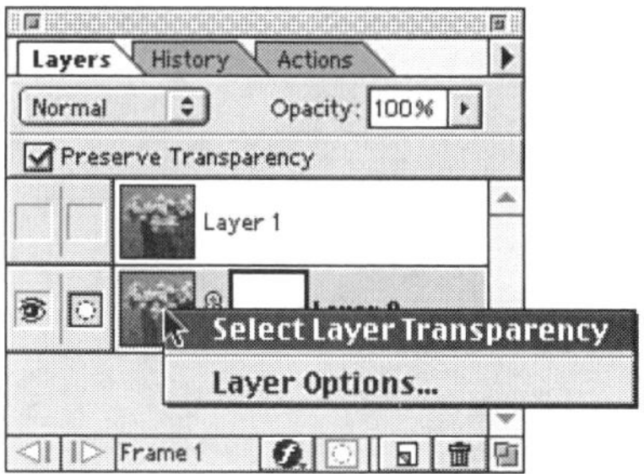

Layer options control.

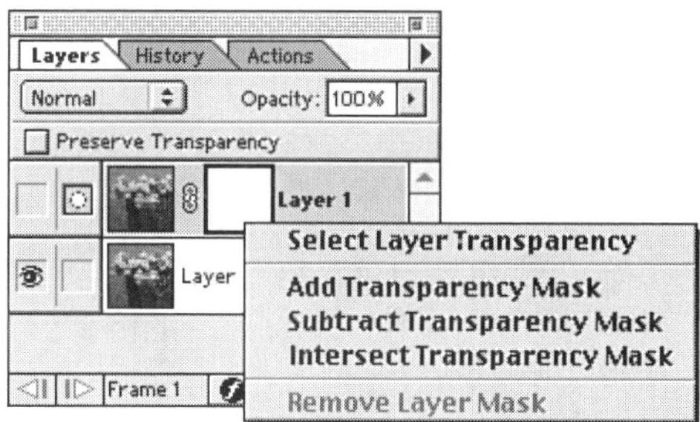

Layer mask control.

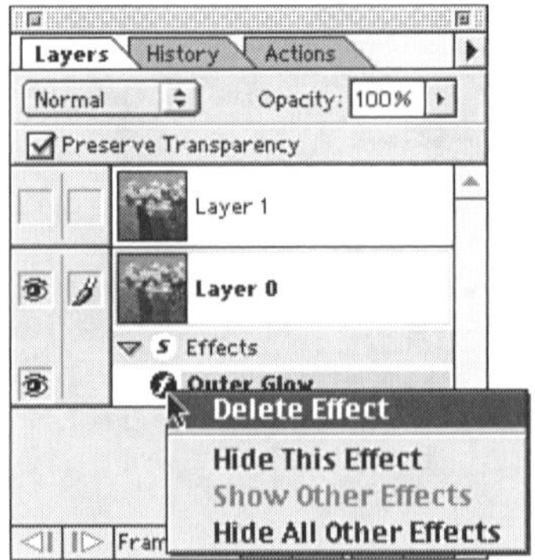

Layer effects control.

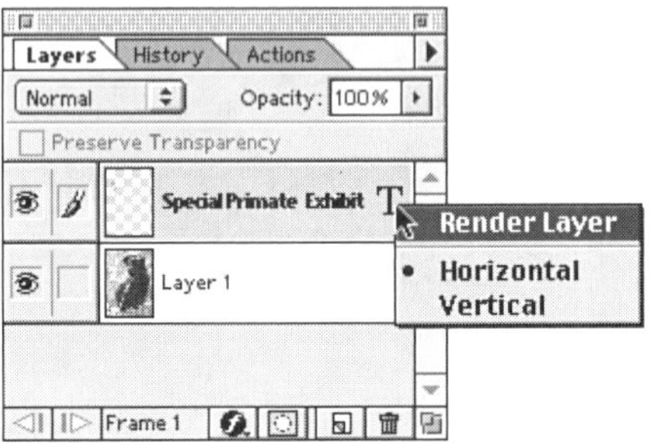

Type Layer control.

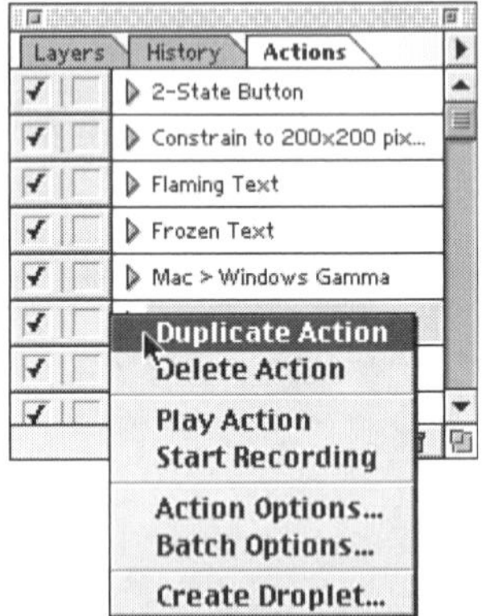

Actions palette.

Photoshop's Best-Kept Secrets

After you've mastered the Top 15 tips on pages 3–7, you'll want to take a whack at Photoshop's best-kept secrets. These are the ones that will make novice users bow down in awe before you, chanting in unison, "I didn't know you could do *that*!" Maybe you already know some of them, but I guarantee that at least one of these puppies will catch your fancy. In no particular order, here they are:

1. **Zoom In or Zoom Out: (Cmd-Plus)[Ctrl+Plus] or (Cmd-Minus) [Ctrl+Minus]**

   These work even better with the plus and minus keys on the numeric keypad—they're easier to find without looking at the keyboard. This shortcut works in dialog boxes, too.

2. **Clear Layer Effects: (Option-Double-click)[Alt+Double-click] effect icon in Layers palette**

   The layer effects are removed in reverse order of their creation. In other words, the most recently created effect is removed first.

3. **Reposition a selection as you create it: Spacebar**

   This one will save you so many steps you'll be wondering how you ever made selections before you knew it. Just don't let go of the mouse button while you're pressing on the spacebar or the selection will be completed—then you can move it but not continue to resize it.

4. **Draw from the center while creating selections: (Option-Drag)[Alt+Drag]**

   It seems simple and so obvious after you try it, and it's particularly useful for elliptical selections. Trying to judge where the "corner" of an elliptical selection will fall is near-impossible—and now you don't have to.

5. **Paint or draw in a straight line: Shift+Click**

   So you can't draw a straight line—so what? Click once with any painting tool at the beginning of the line, and then Shift+Click at the end of the line. Voilà! A straight line.

6. **Reposition type from within the Type dialog box: click and drag in the document window**

   Is it a keyboard shortcut? No! Is it a wicked good timesaver? Yes! Use it and be happy.

7. **Create a protractor: (Option-Drag)[Alt+Drag] an end point**

   The angle change shows up in the Info palette.

8. **Create a duplicate while transforming: (Cmd-Option-T) [Ctrl+Alt+T]**

   This shortcut is great when you're placing multiple, slightly different copies of an element throughout a document. You can do anything you want to the copy—resize it, rotate it, skew it, move it, whatever—without changing the original.

9. **Fade the last filter used: (Cmd-Shift-F)[Ctrl+Shift+F]**

   Filter didn't come out right? Don't undo it, fade it. You can change the opacity and the blend mode of any filter, previewing your changes as you make them.

10. **Reapply the last filter used: (Cmd-F)[Ctrl+F]**

    Why waste time looking for that filter in Photoshop's mare's nest of a Filter menu? If you're applying the same filter repeatedly, to one image or to many, just use this shortcut and take an early coffee break.

Photoshop Index

Symbols

A

B

C

D

E

F

G

H

M

N

O

P

T

U

V

W-Z

ImageReady Index

A

B

C

D

E

F

M

N

O

P

Q-R

S

T

U-V

W-Z